Healing Hidden Hurts:

Leaving the Past and Finding a New Life

GENE APPEL

D1015944

STANDARD
PUBLISHING
Cincinnati, Ohio

Cover design by SchultzWard, Inc.

The Standard Publishing Company, Cincinnati, Ohio.
A division of Standex International Corporation.

01 00 99 98 97 96 95 94   1 2 3 4 5

Library of Congress Cataloging in Publication data:

Appel, Gene.
    Healing hidden hurts : leaving the past and finding a new life / Gene Appel.
    p. cm.
    ISBN 0-7847-0133-4
    1. Suffering--Religious aspects--Christianity.   2. Adjustment (Psychology)--Religious aspects--Christianity.   3. Christian life--1960-   I. Title.
BV4909.A66   1994
248.8'6--dc20   93-37232
                                                    CIP

Contents

Dedication

To Jeremy
Whose beautiful mother became my wife
on January 13, 1993,
Who knows his own hidden hurts,
Who has brought new levels of joy to my life,
Whom I am honored and humbled to call "son,"
And who, I pray, always walks with the Healer,
God's Son.

FOREWORD

Bill Hybels

Every once in a while, I open an envelope and read a letter that compels me to abandon my carefully laid-out schedule for the day and immediately hand write a heart-felt response to the writer. That is precisely how I came to know the author of this book, Gene Appel. Gene had just experienced a not-so-hidden hurt in his life and had decided to take a risk by confiding in me. Our correspondence eventually led to a relationship that has since developed into a close friendship that far transcends ministry.

After a recent time of fellowship with Gene, I felt what the apostle Paul said he felt for Timothy—"a kindred spirit."

Gene is a radical Christ-follower and a passionate pastor. He is a bold proclaimer of God's truth and a gentle conveyor of his grace. He is both a truth seeker and a truth teller.

In this book you will find more than helpful information about life's *Hidden Hurts*. You will feel the tender touch of healing grace from someone who has been there—and survived!

Bill Hybels
Senior Pastor
Willow Creek Community Church

INTRODUCTION

Moving Beyond the Past

Masks. You know what I'm talking about. We're pretty good at wearing them. People ask us, "How you doing?"

"Great!" we say. But we know things aren't great. Beneath our masks lie hurts that we hide and harbor. Sometimes we even try to hide them from ourselves.

Whether the hurt is a broken heart, a guilty conscience, lingering loneliness, harbored hatred, family secrets, or continuing grief—because it's hidden—we often neglect to reach out for help. And often those who could reach out to us and help us walk through the hurt are unaware of our secret pain. We keep it too well hidden from them.

In my first book, *Dream Intruders,* I dealt with the subjects of accidents, terminal illness, being fired, bankruptcy, prodigal children, and divorce. When those dream intruders happen, everybody knows it. They are public crises. The people who can help us move into action quickly. The outpouring of love, cards, and prayers sometimes overwhelms us.

But when hidden hurts simmer in our hearts, the people who could help are often unaware. The hidden hurts may be the residue of a dream intruder that never really got healed. We have managed to survive the crisis, but we continue to feel the fallout. So we go on hurting and hurting—alone and unaware of the resources, people, spiritual guidance, and power for healing that God has put within our reach.

If you are unwilling to remove your mask and be vulnerable with other people and with God, then there's no need for you to read any further. This book can't help you. However, if you are willing to risk being yourself, telling the truth, and opening up the door to the secret passageway leading to your hurts, then maybe you'd like to join me on this journey—leaving the past behind and finding a new life.

Now please understand something—healing hidden hurts is a process and not an instantaneous event. Often it begins by stopping the bleeding. Then some stitches, bandages, and disinfectant are needed while the wound begins to close. Once in a while it gets bumped and reopened before the healing is complete. But eventually healing does come.

Oh, yes—after everything is said and done, there's usually a scar. But rather than being a source for more pain, the scar serves as kind of a badge to honor the Great Physician, the ultimate healer of our hurts.

I'm eager to take this journey with you. Why? Because I've made some journeys down these roads myself. I've gone through the vulnerable experience of removing some of my masks. And I'm beginning to grasp what the great apostle meant when he wrote, "Being confident of this, that he who began a good work in you will carry it on to completion until the day of Christ Jesus" (Philippians 1:6).

CHAPTER ONE

Healing the Hurt of a Broken Heart

I was a freshman in high school.

Her name was Lynnette.

The love bug bit during marching band practice. When I looked at her, I marched a little faster than everybody else.

We had been an item for a few weeks when she was selected attendant for the freshman class during homecoming activities. I was thinking, "Life doesn't get any better than this: Lynnette, freshman class attendant, my girlfriend!" Then she dumped me to go to the homecoming dance with the quarterback of the varsity football team.

They call that puppy love, but I want to tell you: it was real to this puppy!

A broken heart is unreturned love. It's what happens when you make an investment in loving someone, and the investment goes sour. There was no love returned for love given. You risked, and you were burned. You trusted, and you were betrayed.

Max Lucado writes about walking through an old cemetery and coming across the tombstone that marked the body of Grace Lewellen Smith. No date of birth was listed, no date of death. Just the names of her two husbands and this sad epitaph: "Sleeps, but rests not. Loved, but was loved not. Tried to please, but pleased not. Died as she lived—alone."

That grave marks a woman who died with a broken heart. Think of those words, "Loved, but was loved not," and picture the long nights, an empty bed, no response to messages left, the void. Love was given, but no love was exchanged. It was unreturned love.

Certain words and phrases stab at the heart like a knife. And the pain in each is the message of unreturned love. For some, these words and the heartbreak that they cause are too familiar:

"I don't have the same feelings for you that you have for me."

"I just don't love you anymore."

"I never really loved you."

"I'm leaving you."

"There's someone else."

"I want a divorce."

When God made us, he put within us a fantastic capacity to think and feel, giving us the potential for *ecstasy* on the one hand, but, with it, an equal potential for *agony* on the other.

Please remember this: God knows all about a broken heart firsthand. No one has ever suffered more emotional rejection than Jesus—betrayed, denied, and murdered by those he came to love. What a picture of unreturned love. Yet never once did he react or strike back and hurt those who were hurting him. Jesus demonstrates for us that broken hearts are not nearly as important as how we react to broken hearts. Our response determines whether we will get bitter or get better.

This subject is very personal for me. In the biography of Gene Appel, "Surviving a Broken Heart" could be the title of the chapter that begins on October 11, 1989. However, in the midst of it all, I learned that with God's strength you can survive a broken heart.

I know many others are going through it, too. No one is immune. It affects all age groups. Twenty-five percent of the marriages of people in their early fifties end in divorce. One fifth of all divorces involve people over forty who've been married longer than twenty-five years.

If you've never experienced a broken heart, I hope this chapter will help you in knowing how to be more sensitive and how to help hurting family and friends with understanding.

My Broken Heart

I met the young woman who would later become my wife at Bible college. It truly was love at first sight as our eyes met from across a crowded room in the college cafeteria. Pretty romantic, don't you think? Maybe it wasn't true love, but I know I at least loved the sight! There was instant chemistry, and we immediately started dating. It was wonderful. It was never on again, off again, on again, off again. It was just on.

The encounter in the cafeteria was the beginning of a three-year courtship that culminated in our marriage in 1984. Everything seemed perfect. She was from a wonderful Christian family. Not only did we click, but so did our families. We had the fairy-tale wedding and honeymoon.

I was an associate minister in a small midwest town at the time. Just about a year after we were married, when I was twenty-five years old, we accepted the invitation for me to be the senior minister at Central Christian Church in Las Vegas, Nevada. With excitement and anticipation, we made the transition. Both of us sensed God's call to minister in this city where so many people need to know that God loves them.

The next four years were challenging and very demanding in the ministry. The church grew rapidly, I took a number of outside speaking engagements, the staff expanded, and we entered a major building program. The "tyranny of the urgent" always took my attention. I was so closely involved with the trees of my life that I couldn't see the forest. I failed to recognize the toll my pace was taking on our relationship and changes that were taking place in my life.

October 11, 1989, began as an exciting day. In some ways, it marked a finish line for our first four years of ministry in Las Vegas. I keep a journal every day, and this small quote from my journal that morning captures a little bit of the excitement that was in my heart:

This is a day that I've looked forward to for nearly four years. The dedication of our new building is tonight. This is the first time I've ever led through a building program. It's been a challenge. It's been fun. And it's exciting to think about the possibilities that are before us as a congregation right now.

It was a great night as people who had prayed and given sacrificially gathered to dedicate this new facility to be a tool in helping people discover and grow in Christ. If it's possible to be on a mountain, I was there. There are things a lot more important than buildings, but I knew this building was needed and would really assist our ministry.

During the dedication service, the chairman of our elders said some very kind things about my ministry with the church. The congregation graciously let me know of their enthusiastic support with a sustained standing ovation. I'd like to say I took it all in stride and it didn't give me a big head, but that wouldn't be totally true. However, in just a few short hours, God was going to make me face that pride head on and take me from one of the highest highs I had ever known in ministry to the absolute lowest valley I've ever experienced.

When we crawled into bed that night, my wife of almost five years and sweetheart for three years before that would say some things to me that would change my life forever. I didn't write in my journal again until October 20, our fifth wedding anniversary:

I have just celebrated the most painful wedding anniversary I think one could imagine. Nine days ago, the night of October 11, Sharon told me she was leaving me the next day and she was in love with another man. I was shocked. I kept thinking she would say it was a joke.

The night she broke the news to me had been one of the highlights of my life—the dedication of our new facility. While I had been building God's Kingdom, Satan, with my help and her help, had been destroying my marriage.

Two days later I wrote these words to Sharon in a letter:

I'm still numb at the events of the past 11 days. How I could be blind to them for so long is beyond me. To think that two people can live in the same house and know so little about the lives of each other is pretty alarming. I know you must really be hurting. In the midst of my pain I want you to know I still love you with all my heart. I can't describe to you the hurt it is to hear you say you're not sure if you love me anymore. Most of the time in relationships when things get tough most people can say, "But at least we still love each other." It's tough to know maybe we don't even have that.

We have so many great memories of important events in our lives that we have shared together: plays, your high school graduation, my ordination and college graduation, your days at college, choir tour to Boston, trips with your folks, our engagement, our wedding planning, rehearsal, wedding day, and honeymoon to Jamaica. Our first days of marriage, our excitement about moving to Las Vegas. We have so many memories together. How I want to continue the string of memories over the course of the rest of our lives.

Those of you who've walked in those shoes know the emotional war that goes on inside of you when your heart's broken like that. So many emotional extremes rage inside of you. I was just dumbfounded by it all for so long. There were many times in that first year when I'd be taking a nap or daydreaming and would wake up in a sweat thinking, "This must just be a bad dream. This can't be real. This doesn't happen to people like me. This happens to other people. How could this have happened?"

I don't know how to put into words the emotional extremes you go through after experiencing a broken heart. Sometimes you are extremely angry at the people who hurt you. At other times your heart goes out for the people who hurt you. You know that hurting people hurt people, but to let go of the bitterness and release the hurt and to forgive violates your sense of justice. So you try to hold it all in. Only later do you realize if you allow it to fester, it will destroy you.

Thankfully I had a loving church family and the wise counsel of a godly eldership who was patient with me and gave me the space and time I needed to work through what was happening—and I will be forever indebted. I had family members and friends who called, came, visited, and prayed.

I really wanted more than anything in the world to reconcile the relationship. It would have been a wonderful testimony to the power of God and the power of repentance and forgiveness to have been able to tell you my wife had a change of heart and together we rebuilt our marriage and it is better than ever. But that's not how our story ends.

In August of 1990, she filed for a divorce. Several months later, it was final. In what seemed like an unbelievable turn of events, I was now single. "Single again." Fortunately, we had no children who could be hurt in the aftermath, as so often happens.

Since then I've been writing new chapters in my life. I've learned a lot about myself and a lot about God. I hope I've grown a lot. Perhaps one of the greatest things that happened to me is that I learned how much growing I have yet to do in my life. I've been able to overcome the fear of admitting that and talking about it, thus opening the door for more growth to occur.

I know I have a lot yet to learn, but I want to share with you some *do*s and *don't*s I've learned that have helped me find healing for a broken heart.

Don'ts for Healing a Broken Heart

If you really want a broken heart to heal, there will be times when you have to refuse your first impulse. Sometimes the natural thing to do is the wrong thing to do!

#1, Don't Bury Your Hurts

Ephesians 4:26 instructs us, "Do not let the sun go down while you are still angry." But that is just what we do. We don't deal with our anger. We keep sweeping it under the carpet.

This is good advice to those of you who have not experienced a broken heart yet and would like to keep it that way. I know it doesn't seem like a big deal when you bury things a day at a time. But burying hurts like that is what leads people to wake up one day and suddenly realize they don't know each other anymore. It doesn't happen *suddenly*. It happens over the course of a long time of burying hurts, of letting the sun go down while you're still angry.

#2, Don't Pull Out of Life

Naturally, none of us wants to be hurt. So when we get hurt, the first impulse is to pull back into a shell so we cannot be hurt again. Love by its very nature is a risk to be hurt, so we cannot eliminate the risk to be hurt without giving up love. But without love, we are going to hurt even more.

When my world fell apart, I was in such shock that I went into isolation for a few weeks. I wanted to protect any future chance of our reconciliation, so I thought the fewer who knew the details, the better. I did share openly with our elders. Shortly afterwards a brother in Christ sent me a letter that became a turning point in my recovery. I began to open up to some close friends rather than withdrawing. He wrote:

Dear Geno [that's what my close friends call me],

I cannot tell you how much I feel for you at this time, and I wish there were words to describe my sorrow. We are praying daily and thinking about you constantly. You are a dear friend and a constant source of Christian uplifting in our life.

I realize that at a time like this, time to be by yourself and the Lord is most important, but I don't want you to forget that my lines are open for you. I wish at a time like this I could just give you a hug and take over all the pain you are feeling in your heart, but since this is not possible, I would like to share the load with you. For a friend to share the load, this means to be there any time of day or night; I'm here for you pal. I hope you will turn to me for anything you want. Our home is wide open for you, our hearts are open for you. You are like a brother to me and I love you. When you are good and ready, please contact me anytime of day or night, it doesn't matter. We won't stop praying for you, or thinking about you.

Well, I took the risk and made contact. I decided I wasn't going to pull out of life and away from people any longer. And God has given me several close, intimate friends in the intervening time with whom there is unconditional acceptance and confidentiality. And I am grateful. I have deeper, more honest friendships today than I've ever had in my life. It took a broken heart to make me willing to talk about, face, and deal with weaknesses in my own life that I would have been too proud to talk about or too egotistical to even admit before. I encourage those of you close to a brokenhearted person, come alongside of him and make yourself available like that. You can't force yourself on him, but he may open up. And in that confidential encounter there is healing.

#3, Don't Run From Other Good Relationships

I've discovered that the reason a lot of people are unable to show affection and have warm and close relationships is that somewhere in their past they were rejected by someone they loved (maybe even a parent). So, consciously or unconsciously, they made a vow, "Never again will I be hurt like this. Never again will I care enough for anyone to let them hurt me."

But when we say things like that, we are the ones who lose the most. We sit on the sidelines while life passes us by. We withdraw and just go on hurting and hurting and hurting—all alone. We must not allow our emotional hurt to take us out of the mainstream of life.

Don't ever say: "I'll never trust anyone again." "I've been hurt once and never again." "I'll never love anyone again."

I know it's awkward to re-engage in life as a solo when you're used to being part of a duet. I'll never forget my first date after the divorce. I was scared to death! I was especially nervous about being out in public and running into people from my church. We went to a Friday afternoon movie at about 5 P.M. I told her it would work best with my schedule—but really, I'm cheap, and afternoon movies are half-price! We made it through the parking lot and lobby unscathed and entered the dimly lit theater. We saw a row completely empty except for one man on the end. I said, "Let's sit there." She crept in past the man, and then, as I followed, he said—in a voice loud enough for everyone in the theater to hear—"Hey, preacher!" I couldn't believe it. I must have turned ten shades of red. But, today, I can look back at laugh about that experience. As embarrassing as it was, it was a step toward wholeness and having good relationships in my life.

That's a hard step to take, but you dare not run from other good relationships God has for you. If you do, you are going to miss out on many good things God has in store for your future.

#4, Don't Cling to Your Hurt

Hebrews 12:15 says, "Watch out that no bitterness takes root among you, for as it springs up it causes deep trouble, hurting many in their spiritual lives" (*The Living Bible*). The truth is, the more you hold on to hurts, the longer and more intense your hurts will become. (See chapter 4.)

Once in a while I get the feeling as I talk to people that their emotional hurts are like their best friends. They hold on to their hurts as if they just couldn't get along without them. They cling to their hurts as if they were their last few close friends.

We need to release our hurts. If we don't, the hurts will develop into the destroying diseases of hate, resentment and bitterness. It's like a splinter in your finger. As long as it remains, there is a possibility of infection. If left alone, the infection could grow and go up your arm and spread through your body, and even produce blood poisoning that could kill you. That's what holding onto hurts will do to us.

You'll never survive your broken heart as long as you are holding on to resentment, hatred, and bitterness.

Dos for Healing a Broken Heart

On the positive side, the sooner you can start taking action, the better. To delay only leaves the wound wide open for infection.

#1, Do Focus on the Only Person You Can Change—You

Your tendency is to focus on the person who hurt you. You want to excuse yourself and blame the other person.

18

You want to say everything will be all right just as soon as the other person comes around and does the right thing. But getting agitated about what the other person has done to you is useless. One of the hardest lessons I've learned is that I cannot change another person; I can only change myself.

You are not responsible to God for what anyone else does. You are only responsible for yourself.

Focusing on what someone else has done to you rather than on your own attitude and actions is like driving a car while looking only at the rearview mirror. If all you can see is what is behind you, you'll never focus on what is ahead. If you are always looking back, you will crash!

You cannot focus in two different directions at once. That is the reason 1 John 4:20 tells us we cannot love God and hate a brother at the same time.

So focus on the only person you can change, and that's you. Don't focus on the one who hurt you. Don't focus on the past. If you do, you allow that person to rob you of your joy. You will not be able to see the positive things God is trying to bring into your life. Focus on what you can learn and become.

#2. Do Take Advantage of This Graduate School of Life

Broken hearts are one of the greatest schools of higher learning you will ever attend. You're going to learn all kinds of things about yourself. You're going to learn some good things about yourself, and you're going to learn some ugly things.

I think of these difficult times as "desert experiences." Moses spent forty years in the desert. That must have seemed fruitless at the time, but it was preparing him to be the deliverer of the Hebrew people from Egypt. After Paul became a Christian, he didn't just go right into being a successful missionary. There were days in the desert that really built his character and helped him learn things about himself that made him more effective later.

Every broken person learns his own lessons in the desert. Here are some of the lessons I learned:

- I've learned the importance of total truth-telling in relationships, even at the expense of pain and facing ugly things about myself and my relationships.
- I've learned that when you lose everything that's important to you but your relationship to Jesus Christ, he is enough.
- I've learned I had an unhealthy work ethic that was motivated by several factors: insecurity, a need to succeed for my own self-image, and the untimely death of my father when I was fourteen years old. My dad was used greatly by God. When he died prematurely at the age of 52, I put it upon myself not only to fulfill my own ministry for the Lord, but to fulfill the ministry of Leon Appel that was cut short. I placed a mantle on my shoulders that God never intended to be placed there.
- I've learned that God hasn't called me to be anybody but Gene Appel, and he is only going to hold me accountable for the gifts he has given to me—nothing less, nothing more. So I can relax.
- I've learned the importance of balance in life. It's not enough to be spiritually healthy. You need to have parameters to protect your physical, mental, and emotional health as well.
- I've learned the freedom of just being myself in all situations. Trying to maintain an "image" is bondage. Creating a persona for myself that I can't live up to is bondage. So now I just try to be myself wherever I am and whoever I'm with. That feels good!
- I've learned the importance of intimate friendships.

You're probably thinking, "Boy, Gene, you had a lot to learn, didn't you?" I did. And deep down, I have a sense that I'm only just beginning. There's a lifetime of growing God wants to accomplish in my life yet. I hate admitting this, but the ugly truth is I very likely would never have learned these lessons without going through the hidden hurt of a broken heart. I had to be knocked on the side of the head to get my attention. I would like to think I could have grown in some other way, but with the pace my life was moving at the time, I'm not sure I would have ever slowed down long enough to take a second look at these issues.

#3, Do Disinfect the Wound

You say, "How do you do that?" You practice forgiveness. Ephesians 4:31 and 32 says, "Get rid of all bitterness, rage and anger, brawling and slander, along with every form of malice. Be kind and compassionate to one another, forgiving each other, just as in Christ, God forgave you." Colossians 3:13 says, "Be ready to forgive, never hold grudges. Remember, the Lord forgave you, so you must forgive others."

Another side of my situation is the struggle of hate and bitterness I had toward the other man. He and I had been friends; we played tennis together regularly; he professed to be a brother in Christ. What kind of man steals another man's wife? Do you know what I wanted to do to him? Let me just say if I had done it, I would have been arrested and put in jail for a very long time.

Instead, let me tell you about what became a turning point for me. In my quiet time one morning, I was reading from Proverbs 25. I came to verse 21: "If your enemy is hungry, give him food to eat; if he is thirsty, give him water to drink." When I read that, I knew I needed to do more than forgive in my spirit. I needed to take positive action toward my enemy. So I sat down and wrote him a letter. Along with the letter, I sent him a book that had been instrumental in my life, *Honest to God—Becoming an Authentic Christian.* I wrote inside the jacket of the book, "My prayer is that an authentic Christian faith will be the mark of your life. And in return that it will mark others."

From that day forward I've prayed for him regularly. Honestly, that's been one of the most difficult things I've ever done in my life. You say, "Gene, has it brought about a change in his life?" I don't know, but I do know that it's brought about a great change in mine. Take it from someone who knows: if we hold on to hurt, it turns into hate. We need to disinfect the wound, forgive, and let it go.

#4, Do Allow God to Heal Your Broken Heart

Jesus said, "Come to me all who are weary and burdened, and I will give you rest." Let me tell you, he was telling the truth. He really does give rest. You'll never know that until you decide to trust him.

Psalm 34:18 says, "The Lord is close to the brokenhearted and saves those who are crushed in spirit." God wants to help you move forward in life. And God can do that because he understands divorce very well. Do you know why? Because God himself is divorced! He says in Jeremiah 3:8, "I gave faithless Israel her certificate of divorce and sent her away because of all her adulteries." You see, God knows the pain of divorce. He knows what it's like to have your heart broken by an unfaithful party. He knows what it's like not to want a divorce, but to have it happen anyway. And he knows how to move forward. He knows that failure in marriage does not make you a failure in life.

The truth is, you'll never experience the closeness of God and you'll never find the power to heal your broken heart unless you let go of the situation and let God restore you.

Maybe you don't think you can ever get over your broken heart. Friend, that's the reason you need Jesus Christ. Philippians 4:13 says, "I can do all things through Christ who strengthens me." You can even find healing for the hurt. You can even forgive someone you thought you never could. You can even find happiness in ways and places you didn't expect to find it.

Epilog

I cannot close this chapter without telling you an exciting postscript to my story. After a time of recovery, healing, and

restoring wholeness to my life, God brought a beautiful, sweet woman into my life at a time and place I least expected it.

That surprise spilled over onto our church family at a Wednesday night service on January 13, 1993. My good friend Mike Breaux was scheduled to preach, but instead, he got up and said this to our church family:

"I have two major announcements tonight. First, Gene Appel and Barbara Cowan are engaged!" The place erupted with approving applause. Then Mike added: "And the second announcement is—you're at their wedding!" There was shock, disbelief, and then happiness.

On that special night, the church family who had walked with me through the valleys joined Barbara and me for a walk on the mountain top. What a testimony to the amazing grace of God! That grace can heal your broken heart, too.

Jesus loves with an everlasting love. His love never fails; it never disappoints. You will never see your love for Jesus unreturned. He can help you move forward, slowly, steadily, and one step at a time if you'll let him.

Take it from someone who knows!

Questions for Discussion

1. This book is about "hidden" hurts. Is there some way to see behind the masks and diagnose our friends' hidden hurts, or do we have to wait until they drop the masks on their own? If so, how?
2. If you suspect a friend is hurting, what if anything can you do if he or she has not asked for your help?
3. The author describes two cases in which his heart was broken. Once was in high school; the second was when his wife divorced him. What makes the second more significant than the first? How should our response to the high-school student who has been jilted by his first

"puppy love" differ from our response to the adult who has lost a mate?

4. The day the author discovered his wife was planning to leave had been an especially good day until then. Do you think it is common for mountain-top experiences to be followed so closely by heartbreaks? Why or why not?

5. How do you think this kind of situation affects the heart-break? Does it increase the pain by the stark contrast, or does it make the pain easier to bear? Why?

6. What are the four *don'ts* for dealing with a broken heart? Which one do you think is the most important? Why?

7. What are the four *dos* for dealing with a broken heart? Which one do you think is the most important? Why?

8. What broken-heart experiences have you had? Can you list any positive lessons you learned from them?

9. Could you pray for someone who has broken your heart? Why or why not? If not, how can you grow in grace to be able to do so?

CHAPTER TWO

Healing the Hurt of a Guilty Conscience

2 Samuel 11, 12

"What is a guilty conscience?" That question was posed to a couple of six-year-olds, and their definitions are hard to improve upon. A six-year-old girl said, "A guilty conscience is a pot inside of you that burns if you are not good." A six-year-old boy said, "A guilty conscience is feeling bad when you kick girls or little dogs."

A guilty conscience occurs when we violate our sense of proper conduct. Our inside says that it's wrong. Our conscience says we should be ashamed of ourselves. And so, like these children, we go through life feeling bad. We go through life with a pot inside of us that is burning.

Sometimes we try to cover it up, to act as if nothing is bothering us. We men seem especially eager to hide the hurt of a guilty conscience. But I've had the opportunity to be with a number of men in those rare moments when they dropped their masks and talked about what was happening inside of them. I'm always amazed with how much guilt they carry, often about things that happened years ago.

Nobody likes the feeling of a guilty conscience. We do everything we can to avoid it, but we all feel it because nobody's perfect. The only way to avoid a guilty conscience is never to do anything wrong. But we all do.

So you and I carry a load of baggage called guilt. The memory may be as fresh as last night, or it may be of an event that occurred way back in the dark recesses of your past. But it still dogs you, haunts you, and causes you to lose sleep.

There are many examples in the Bible of people who found release from their guilty consciences. For instance, in 2 Timothy 1:3 the apostle Paul thanked God that he served him with a "clear conscience." Yet this same Paul also referred to himself as the "chief of sinners" (1 Timothy 1:15). Did you know that Paul was a murderer? He was there giving approval to the stoning of Stephen (Acts 8:1). How is it possible for a persecutor and murderer of Christians to say years later, "I have a clear conscience"? How did Paul find release? That's what this chapter is about.

The Bible has good news for guilt carriers. It teaches that you can find healing and be released. Yet surprisingly, very few people experience that freedom, even though it is closer to them than they might think.

I want to use David as the backdrop for these observations. David found healing for a guilty conscience that some might have thought incurable. I'm not talking about just any old David. This was the shepherd boy who wrestled lions and bears. This was the young giant killer. This was the decorated military strategist. This was David the influential king. This was David the poet, the author, the husband, the daddy, the man after God's own heart! Men like David don't commit tabloid-worthy sins, do they?

Of course, they do. And, of course, he did. Ironically, at the time it happened, David had been on a spiritual roll with God like few other people have ever experienced. He had been fully devoted to God, and God had blessed that

commitment. David would praise God for his blessing, and then God would bless more. So David would praise him more and God would bless more. This growing cycle of David's praise and God's blessing seemed to be non-stop.

But one moonlit night, everything changed.

_____

The Cause of a Guilty Conscience

In 2 Samuel 11:1, we find that is was the spring of the year, the time when kings normally go off to war, but this year was different. Maybe prosperity was making David soft. This year he stayed home. And it was on one of those lazy nights that David couldn't sleep.

> One evening David got up from his bed and walked around on the roof of the palace. From the roof he saw a woman bathing. The woman was very beautiful, and David sent someone to find out about her (2 Samuel 11:2, 3).

This woman in the bathtub next door was so beautiful that she made David forget that he was a king, a spiritual leader, a husband, a father, and a very godly man. It didn't seem like such a big deal. He was all alone, and everyone else was gone. He could just have a cheap one-night stand, and that would be the end of it. No one would ever find out, and he'd just go right on in his walk with God as if nothing had ever happened. But David's simple second look at the beautiful bathing woman was the beginning of a scandal that grew to gigantic proportions.

To make a long, sensual story short (and some of you are thinking, "Don't skip the sensual part!"), David sent for the woman, whose name was Bathsheba, and he went to bed with her. He committed adultery. *Adultery* is going to bed with someone else's wife. God doesn't like that—and neither does the husband if he finds out!

Immediately there was a problem.

The woman conceived and sent word to David, saying, "I am pregnant" (2 Samuel 11:5).

David had to come up with a cover-up plan. First, he set up the murder of Bathsheba's husband Uriah in such a way that it looked as if he were killed in battle. He died a war hero. Then the rest of David's plan unfolded, and he thought the situation was over and done with.

When Uriah's wife heard that her husband was dead, she mourned for him. After the time of mourning was over, David had her brought to his house, and she became his wife and bore him a son (2 Samuel 11:26, 27).

Now the plan was complete. David had murdered the competition, his girlfriend performed the appropriate public mourning for her dead husband, and David moved his bathing beauty into the palace. They had a child. They pretended everything was okay. Now they could live happily ever after. Right?
Wrong.

But the thing David had done displeased the Lord (2 Samuel 11:27).

There's the cause of a guilty conscience. Did you catch it? It's knowing that you have done something that has displeased the Lord.
A million different things can give us guilt. It doesn't have to be something major and scandalous. One time I had just finished a baptism and went into the changing room at our church building. Dripping wet, I reached for a towel, and you'll never guess what it said. Right there at Central Christian Church in great big letters it said, "HOLIDAY INN." I laughed to myself as I began wondering about the story behind that towel. I envisioned a scenario in which a

person was sitting at home feeling guilty every time he opened the linen closet and looked at that Holiday Inn towel. He probably thought, "I'll just throw it out." But then he was afraid the people who picked up the trash would see it and report him and he'd go to jail. So to ease his conscience, he slipped it among our towels at church one day when no one was looking.

Now my experience tells me that a large percentage of people are dealing with guilt over much larger issues than towels lifted on a summer vacation or driving two or three miles an hour over the speed limit. I say that because, as most any counselor can tell you, people are seldom as good as they seem. I know I'm not as good as I probably seem to a lot of people. And you know the same is probably true for you.

Allow me to list some of the reasons behind the guilt that people have come carrying into my office more frequently than you would imagine.

- Unkept marriage vows, just like David, just like Bathsheba.
- The guilt of an abortion, which seemed like the right thing to do at the time because it could prevent embarrassment. Mom and Dad would never have to know. There wouldn't be another fatherless baby in the world. But now the emotional scar is deep.
- Some carry the guilt of embezzlement. Stealing from the company. Stealing from a family member or friend. They ask, "Can I ever be released from this guilty conscience?"
- Some carry the guilt of homosexual behavior or even one homosexual experience long ago.

When it comes right down to it the cause of David's guilty conscience, the cause of your guilty conscience, and the cause of my guilty conscience is displeasing the Lord—another name for it is sin.

Now let's be honest in saying that there is much initial pleasure in sin. That's why we do it. However, after the initial act of pleasure, we find ourselves enslaved to a guilty conscience.

And the real agony starts to set in.

The Fallout of a Guilty Conscience

The fallout of a guilty conscience falls two ways, inside and outside. Inside, you have to figure some way to silence the voice of rebuke that keeps haunting you. Outside, you have to make sure no one discovers your secret. An arsenal of defense mechanisms isn't enough.

Deception

David's fallout involved a life of deception. He couldn't be honest with his family, his military personnel, himself, or with God.

When you're involved in a sin like adultery, you lie to everybody. You worry, you hope, you cry, you look over your shoulder, you hope nobody finds out. You put up a great front and wear a convincing mask. You go through all of life's normal motions. You go to work, you go to bed, you pray at dinner, you pay the bills, you go to church, you take your kids to see *Snow White*. That's all on the outside. Inside you hurt.

In Psalm 32 David tells us what he felt like carrying this fallout. He lost weight, he groaned, he hurt, he felt heavy. He always felt tired. No matter how much sleep he got—he was still tired. And in his attempt to hide things, David foolishly committed murder, only digging himself into a deeper hole.

You may be able to hide what's going on outside, but inside you hurt. Your guilty conscience tears you up.

In Shakespeare's *Macbeth*, Lady Macbeth and her husband conspire to murder the king. After the act has been committed, her guilty conscience overwhelms her. Even though her hands aren't physically bloody, when she looks at her hands all she can see is the blood of the king. Her agony spills forth as she talks in her sleep, "What, will these hands ne'er be clean? . . . Here's the smell of the blood still. All the perfumes of Arabia will not sweeten this little hand. Oh, oh, oh!"

Maybe like Lady Macbeth you are going through life, pretending everything is okay, but you're in bondage to that guilty conscience. The Bible says, "You may be sure that your sin will find you out" (Numbers 32:23).

A carpet layer was finishing a job when he reached to get a cigarette from his pocket and discovered his pack of cigarettes was gone. He looked down, and underneath the carpet was a little lump. He realized what he had done. He looked one way and then the other. The carpet was already fastened down, so he took his hammer and just flattened it out, thinking nobody would know. When he went to take his tools out to the truck, there was his pack of cigarettes on the dashboard. He came back inside, where the woman of the house was frantic, screaming, "Has anybody seen my canary?"

Your sins will find you out.

Do you recall the scene in the upper room, at the last meal that Jesus shared with his disciples before he was arrested and taken to be crucified? Judas, the deceiver, was there just acting as if everything were normal. Judas had been able to hide the deception in his life from the rest of the group. He had fooled a lot of people. But he could not fool Jesus. Judas had sold out a friend, betrayed his Savior, and deceived his partners for thirty pieces of silver. None of the other disciples even seemed to notice when Jesus told Judas as he got up to leave, "What you are about to do, do quickly." They had no idea what Judas was leaving to do.

Maybe you have successfully deceived those around you as Judas deceived the other 11. Remember that though you may be deceiving everybody else, Jesus knows what's going on in your life. You may have everybody fooled, but not him. Right now at this moment he sees you and me as we really are. He sees what we are when no one else is looking.

Passing the Buck

At some point, the deception almost always fails. Then we need a new tactic. We need to relieve ourselves of the responsibility. We blame others! This is as old as the Garden of Eden, where Adam took it like a man and blamed his wife. "She did it. It's not really my fault." Today it's almost fashionable to say, "It's the fault of my parents, —my boyfriend, —my spouse."

"The devil made me do it."

"It was her idea."

"I got loaded and didn't even know what I was doing."

Rationalization

If we can't escape the blame, then we rationalize: "It's no big deal."

"It doesn't hurt anybody."

"Only this one time."

Do you know what *rationalize* means? It means "rational lies." You rationalize when you try to convince your mind that something is right when you know in your heart it's wrong.

Suppression

Sometimes we attempt to deal with our guilt by suppression. We think, "If I don't admit my guilt, I won't feel guilty; so I just won't think about it." But that never works. It's like trying to keep ten tennis balls submerged in a swimming pool. Just when you get a couple down, one over here pops up. You push it down and two over there pop up. You can't submerge guilt for any period of time.

Distractions

Some of us try to deal with our guilt through distractions. We get so busy with our work, hobbies, family, and volunteer work that at night we plop into bed, sleep, and then hit the pavement running first thing in the morning. But the next time you slow down for just one minute, your guilt overwhelms you.

Isolation

Sometimes we handle guilt through isolation. We avoid the places and the people that remind us of the issue that has never been resolved. This is the reason many people won't go to church. Inside they're saying, "If I go to church, I'll have to think about spiritual issues, and that will remind me of this baggage I'm carrying in my life that needs to be taken care of."

Escape

Others try to handle their guilty conscience through escapism. When they feel guilty, they pop a pill, snort some coke, have a drink, smoke a joint, or go on a gambling binge. They do anything to escape. They go out and have fun. But when they come back down, they've still got the guilt.

You are only deceiving yourself if you think any of these ways will cure your guilty conscience. They only make it worse.

And the guilt is even more intense for those of you who have known the joy of walking with Jesus Christ in your life. You know what is to be forgiven and to be walking consistently toward Jesus. But now you know you're out of fellowship. You don't want to pray. You can't read your Bible. You're not about to expose yourself to a small group. So you avoid the very things that God could use to start bringing about the healing in your life.

While guilt is heavy, we need to understand that it is also healthy. Guilt is a sign that our conscience is still alive. It's a sign that God still loves us. It's a sign that the Holy Spirit is actively trying to work in our lives.

The Cure for a Guilty Conscience

If you've tried all of those other avenues for dealing with a guilty conscience, if you're tired of the deception with others and with yourself, then I want to show you the only path to healing that really works. The cure for a guilty conscience is as simple as 1, 2, 3, 4.

1: Come to Christ and Confess Your Sin

David lived successfully in his deception for a long time, but eventually things started to unravel. People didn't trust David anymore. His son died. His grown-up son started a war to dethrone his dad and ended up getting killed—speared while hanging from a limb by his hair. Who would have thought that one night in bed with a neighbor-lady could have caused all this trouble?

After being confronted by his friend and confidant, Nathan, David decided enough was enough. He got down on his knees and prayed. If you've read the Psalms, you realize that David could be pretty flowery in his prayers. But this time his prayer was different. It wasn't long or flowery. David couldn't have been much more to the point than he was with this simple three-word prayer found in 2 Samuel 12:13, "I HAVE SINNED."

David confessed his sin to God. He confessed his sin to his spiritual mentor. He told his wife he had sinned. He told his family he had sinned. And God forgave him.

It is so important that you understand that forgiveness of sin is reserved only for those who come to Christ and confess. Look at how *The Living Bible* paraphrases Romans 3:23, 24, "Yes, all have sinned; all fall short of God's glorious ideal; yet now God declares us 'not guilty' of offending him if we trust in Jesus Christ, who in his kindness freely takes away our sins."

When Jesus died on the cross, his last words were, "It is finished." What was finished? The payment for our sins was made so that we could be released from our guilty consciences. The Greek for the phrase "It is finished" is just one word, *"tetelestai."* *Tetelestai* was the word on a stamp, and when somebody had paid off a bill at a store, they would stamp it *"tetelestai,"* meaning "Paid in full." When somebody had been in prison and finished serving his term, they would stamp on his prison release papers, *"tetelestai— paid in full."* And when Jesus died on the cross, he said, *"Tetelestai—it is paid in full."*

You can't earn that. You don't have to say, "God, if you'll forgive me, I'll read my Bible every day. I'll give 20% of my income to the church. I'll even work in the church's Junior-high department. I'm really serious, God."

Jesus says, "It's already paid for."

If you want to find the cure for your guilty conscience, it begins by coming to Christ and confessing your sin. God is ready to forgive you. In fact, I would venture to say that God is more ready to forgive you than you are to ask him for forgiveness.

Nehemiah 9:17 says, "But you are a God of forgiveness, always ready to pardon" (*The Living Bible*).

First John 1:9 says, "If we confess our sins, he is faithful and just and will forgive us our sins and purify us from all unrighteousness." So don't unnecessarily hold on to guilt today. If you want to be released from your guilty conscience, come to Christ and confess your sin.

2: Thank God for His Forgiveness

Sometimes our guilt is so heavy that we keep asking for forgiveness when we've already received it. Instead of continually asking for forgiveness, we need to continually thank God for the forgiveness we have already received.

If you are having trouble accepting the fact that God has forgiven your sin, consider these words from God: "For I will forgive their wickedness and will remember their sins no more" (Jeremiah 31:34).

"Their sins and lawless acts I will remember no more" (Hebrews 10:17).

Once sin has been forgiven, God forgets it. He remembers it no more. First Corinthians 13:4 says love "keeps no record of wrongs." God chooses to forget every sin, every mistake you ever make, once you confess it to him.

A priest in the Philippines committed a sin during his seminary days that bugged him to death. He lived constantly in the black fog of a guilty conscience. Even though he had asked for forgiveness many times, he still felt guilty and carried this burden for years and years. A lady in his church claimed that God spoke directly to her. He was very skeptical of that, so he said, "If God really talks to you directly, the next time he says hello, ask him, 'What sin did my priest commit in seminary?'" A few days later she showed up again and he asked her, "Did you ask God about my sin?"

She said, "Yes."

He asked, "What did he say?"

She replied, "God said 'I don't remember.'"

Whether God actually spoke to her or not, she at least got that part right! If you were to commit a sin in the morning, confess it in the afternoon, and die tonight, you could go before God and say, "Now God, about that sin I committed this morning," and he would say, "What sin?"

If you've come to Christ, if you've confessed, "God, I blew it, I made a mistake. It was wrong. It was sin. I ask your forgiveness"—he forgives and forgets. So accept God's forgiveness and thank him.

A little boy was visiting the Washington Monument. He looked up at a policeman standing there, and he said, "I'd like to buy this."

The policeman thought he'd have a little fun with the boy, so he said, "How much you got?"

The boy pulled out the loose change in his pocket and said, "I've got $1.75."

The policeman said, "That's not enough."

The boy looked dejected. And then the policeman said, "Son, you need to understand three things. Number 1, you could never afford to buy this monument. It is priceless.

Number 2, it's not for sale. But—number 3—if you're a citizen of the United States, it already belongs to you, because it belongs to the people of the United States."

God's forgiveness is like that. It's priceless. You could never buy forgiveness from God. It cost Jesus his life. You could never earn it, because it's not for sale. But if you have come to Christ and confessed your sins, then forgiveness is already yours; so thank God for it.

3: Remember That Pain Is Normal

After God has forgiven you, he's not going to punish you, but there are natural consequences that come from our actions. We really do reap what we sow.

In the fallout of David's sin, he lost his baby and his grown-up son. His kids never got over the shame of what their father had done. Bathsheba never forgot how David murdered her first husband. His people never forgot how their king disappointed them. While David will always be remembered as Israel's greatest king, he will also be remembered as history's most notorious adulterer.

Now the pain we experience after forgiveness is easier than guilt, but it's still painful. There's the pain of embarrassment, shame, disappointment and sorrow. So remember when the pain hits that it's normal and it will not last forever.

4: Rebuild Your Life

Start heading in a new direction. Rebuild trust; rebuild relationships; rebuild credibility; rebuild your family.

After Jesus had forgiven the woman caught in the act of adultery in John 8:11, he said to her, "Go, and sin no more." In other words, "Go; rebuild your life." No matter how much failure there has been in your past, through the grace of Jesus Christ, you can begin rebuilding your life today. The day I stop believing that is the day I will stop preaching.

I think one of the greatest testimonies of the church I serve in Las Vegas is that it is full of hundreds of people who are examples that God rebuilds broken lives.

The same God that has helped them and me rebuild our lives is the same God that can give you relief from your guilty conscience. Real relief. Eternal relief. Not just a temporary fix.

The central message of the Bible is that God loves you and wants to forgive you. He knows everything about you and *still* loves you!

Today could be the day that you straighten things out with him. Today could be the day you find healing for your guilty conscience. You could come to Christ and say, "Wipe my slate clean. Give me a fresh start. I give my life to you."

Release it to God. Let it out. Then exhale and breathe a sigh of relief.

Isn't God amazing? He does for us what we could never do for ourselves. Our greatest need is forgiveness and his greatest gift is a forgiver named Jesus.

Questions for Discussion

1. The author says, "A guilty conscience occurs when we violate our sense of proper conduct." What is the source of "our sense of proper conduct"? If that sense is flawed, what happens to the reliability of one's conscience?
2. The author suggests that men are more likely to try to hide the affects of a guilty conscience. Do you agree? Why or why not?
3. In David's deception to cover up his adultery, he became guilty of even greater sin—murder. Do you think this is the usual result, covering up one sin leads to greater sin? If so, why is the cover-up so common?
4. The seven stages of fallout—deception, passing the buck, rationalization, suppression, distractions, isolation, and

escape—seem to be progressive. As each one fails, the person moves to the next. What does this suggest about the need to deal with a guilty conscience quickly?

5. Do you think a discerning friend can recognize the fallout of a guilty conscience even if she does not know her friend has done something wrong? What should you do if you suspect a friend is covering something and suffering from a guilty conscience? What should you do if you *know* a friend has done something wrong? (See Matthew 18:15-20; Galatians 6:1, 2; Jude 22, 23.)

6. Of the four steps in the "cure" for a guilty conscience—come to Christ and confess your sin, thank God for his forgiveness, remember that pain is normal, and rebuild your life—which is the most difficult? Why?

7. In which step is the support of Christian friends most helpful? Why?

CHAPTER THREE

Healing the Hurt of Lingering Loneliness

2 Timothy 4:9-18

Lonely. It sounds so desperate.

Maybe because it is!

Ours is a society filled with lonely people. Many of us are lonely and don't even know why. Others think they have it figured out, but their attempts to cure their loneliness leave them feeling as lonely as ever. Some single people get married because they are lonely, and then a few years later they get divorced for the same reason.

Most of us would never admit it, but inside many of us are saying, "I'm so lonely, it hurts." There are 70% more Americans living alone today than were twenty years ago. The infamous "900 number" phone services are flourishing today, taking in large sums of money, because they prey on lonely people who just want someone to talk to.

Loneliness happens when we feel like, "Nobody really cares about me. Nobody really knows me. Nobody really understands what goes on inside of me."

As the apostle Paul neared the end of his life, he found himself imprisoned in Rome, facing a death sentence, and coping with the hurt of loneliness. Paul was a dying man. At this difficult time, he wrote a letter to his good young friend Timothy and urged Timothy to come visit him.

I think there's a hint of desperation in his voice as Paul pleads with Timothy in 2 Timothy 4:9, "Do your best to come to me quickly." Paul was lonely.

The Surprises of Loneliness

Doesn't it surprise you a little bit that the great apostle Paul was lonely? The Beatles asked, "All the lonely people, where do they all come from?" Surprisingly, they come from every walk of life. Loneliness affects all of us at one time or another. Paul is an example that loneliness strikes three groups of people that you might think would never be lonely. If these people can be lonely, if Paul could be lonely, then no one is immune.

Loneliness Strikes Those Who Are Surrounded by People

Paul was not alone, but he was lonely. There were other prisoners around. There were guards in the prison. And even Luke, the author of the gospel of Luke and the book of Acts, was there with him. Yet he says: "Only Luke is with me" (2 Timothy 4:11).

If I were Luke, I think I might be offended by that comment. That would be like my wife's saying, "It's only Gene with me."

"Only"?

Maybe Paul was just getting tired of Luke. I think it was Mark Twain who said, "Friends are like fish, after three days they start to stink." On the other hand, there may have been no negative emotions in the statement. Paul and Luke may both have been eager to see a new face, to hear a firsthand report from the churches, to share some expanded fellowship.

You see, you can be surrounded by even hundreds of people and still be lonely. The problem of loneliness is not as much isolation as it is insulation. We insulate ourselves—or others insulate themselves—with plastic smiles, so we never really draw close to the people around us. It's very possible to be constantly around other people in your work, at school, at church, in your family, and still be lonely. It's not the number of people around you that determines the presence or absence of loneliness. It's your relationship to them.

Loneliness Strikes Successful People

Paul had been so successful in his lifetime. Everywhere he went, people flocked to hear him speak. There's probably never been a missionary, preacher, and author more effective and famous than Paul. Yet this successful person was lonely.

We often assume that successful people couldn't possibly be lonely. After all, they're strong, they encourage others. But when you're at the top of the field in your own area of expertise, there's often a loneliness that accompanies your success.

H.G. Wells was a great author, but he wrote, "I am 65 and I am lonely, and I have never known peace." Pyotr Tchaikovsky was a successful composer but wrote, "None but the lonely heart can feel my anguish."

Albert Einstein, the successful scientist and theorist, said, "It is strange to be known so universally and yet be so lonely."

Loneliness Strikes Christian People

We sometimes reason that if we really have a personal relationship with Christ, if we really walk with him, we'll never be lonely. Right? Not according to Paul. Being a Christian did not exempt him from feeling lonely.

Sometimes you meet apparently pious people who say, "Well, I just need Jesus. After all, he never leaves me or forsakes me." That sounds nice, but even Jesus needed close intimate relationships with people. God created us not only for community with him, but for community with each other. It was God who said, "It is not good for man to be alone." As essential as a personal relationship with Jesus Christ is every day, it can't be a substitute for other human relationships.

In spite of the fact that Paul was a Christian and Christ was with him, he was still lonely. So if you're a Christian, don't think that something is spiritually wrong with you when you feel lonely. You're in good company with the apostle Paul.

But what is the root of our loneliness?

Why Are We Lonely?

I find at least three things that caused Paul's loneliness. The first one is probably the most common—

Separation

Paul was confined in prison and separated from practically all of his close, intimate friends. Here was a man who loved to travel, who never stayed in one place for more than three years, and he was chained to his cell and separated from his friends. No wonder he was lonely.

Just think about the different circumstances that separate people. For instance, *death separates*. I remember talking on the phone to my mother one Valentine's Day. She said she had been thinking about my dad all day—yet Dad had died over fifteen years before. I heard the loneliness in her voice when she said, "You know, there will never be another man like your dad."

Divorce separates. Divorces are always followed by intense times of loneliness. What used to be close friendships are awkward now. Most of your friends were other couples, but now you're a one-person team, and you feel so isolated.

City-life separates. I don't know if your city is like the city I live in, but Las Vegas is full of condominiums, high-rise apartments, town houses, block walls between yards, and gated neighborhoods. That spells separation. People have never lived so close together, yet felt so far apart.

Moving separates. One in every five Americans moves each year. Four out of five residents of Las Vegas have come from some place else, leaving families, friends, and memories behind. It's lonely when you pull up stakes and come into a new city where you have no roots. All of your lasting and meaningful relational ties are elsewhere.

The military separates. Just ask some people who have spouses or children or grandchildren serving in the armed forces around the world or away on temporary duty assignments. Listen to the loneliness in the voices of some of our troops when they send back greetings to their families on TV during the holiday season.

Every stage of life has factors that cause separation. A child is lonely when he has no one to play with. A teenager is lonely when his peers reject him. An adult is lonely when he has no one with whom to share dreams and joys. Parents are lonely when the kids move out. An elderly person is lonely when he no longer feels needed. When elderly people complain that they feel unloved and unwanted, that is not just the ramblings of senile people. Seven of every ten people who live in convalescent-type homes never get a visit from anybody. Never.

Opposition

Paul said:

Alexander the metalworker did me a great deal of harm. The Lord will repay him for what he has done. You too should be on your guard against him, because he strongly opposed our message (2 Timothy 4:14, 15).

Not only was Paul getting old and sitting there lonely in prison, but he had been directly attacked. We don't know what Alexander did to Paul. Maybe he had brought false accusations against him in court. Maybe he had been turning people against Paul. Perhaps he had challenged the validity of Paul's preaching.

But when you are vigorously opposed, whether it's in court, in your work, in your family, or in school, it is a lonely feeling.

Do you remember when you were in grade school how quickly you could go from being everybody's friend to nobody's friend? Kids can say some of the cruelest things. All of the sudden they can point their finger at you and say, "You're not our friend anymore." That kind of rejection is painful.

Desertion

People whom Paul had thought he could trust and lean on had deserted him when he needed them most. You can hear the loneliness in his words: "For Demas, because he loved this world, has deserted me and has gone to Thessalonica. . . . At my first defense, no one came to my support, but everyone deserted me" (2 Timothy 4:10, 16). Even some of Paul's loyal co-workers—Crescens, Titus, and Tychicus—had inadvertently added to Paul's loneliness because they were on missions to Galatia, Dalmatia, and Ephesus (2 Timothy 4:10, 12). But even worse were the desertions.

It seems unbelievable that when the pressure was really on Paul, everyone deserted him. No one took the witness stand in his defense. He was abandoned when he needed people most. That must have been hard. But Paul discovered, as you can discover, that loneliness is not fatal. You can find healing for your lingering loneliness.

The Cure for Loneliness

Maybe we first ought to identify a few things that won't cure it. Maybe you've tried one or all of these.

False Cures

Workaholism Won't Make It Disappear. Some people use work as a defense mechanism in order not to deal with their loneliness. They run around saying, "I'd rather burn out than rust out." They have a sign on their desk that says, "Thank God it's Monday." A workaholic, who has achieved practically every level of success possible in his particular field but has failed miserably in his personal life, told me one day, "My goal is to have just one successful relationship before my life is over."

Materialism Won't Cure Loneliness. Some people reason, "If I just get enough things, then I'll be happy." But that won't work. If you were put on a tropical island and told, "You can have anything you want except human contact," how long do you think you'd be happy? Not very long. That's the reason solitary confinement is the most devastating form of punishment. That's the reason dads who give their kids everything but never have any time to spend with them eventually find their kids bitter and withdrawn. People need people.

Escapism Won't Cure Loneliness. Many have tried to escape their loneliness through an affair, alcohol, or chemicals. Some have tried to escape to a fantasy world of reading novels and watching movies and television. But when the fantasy trip is over, the loneliness is still there.

Black Tie, Sit Down and Feel Sorry for Me, Pity-Parties Also Fail to Cure Loneliness. I know a lot about this one. We grovel about how bad things are. We can be negative as you've never seen negative! Paul, however, refused to sit around and mope. He didn't say, "Poor me, poor me." He didn't complain, "God, is this what I get for thirty years of ministry? Is this my reward for starting lots of churches, for being the person most single-handedly responsible for the spread of Christianity throughout the Roman world? Is this what I get—to die in loneliness in a damp prison in Rome?"

If anybody had a reason to throw a pity party, it was Paul. But, instead, he gave his situation over to the Lord and said, "The Lord will repay him for what he has done" (2 Timothy 4:14). That's not a desire for revenge. That's not harbored hatred. That's just turning the situation over to the Lord and letting go of the negativism.

The True Cure

We all know what won't cure loneliness, but what will? Here are four positive actions lonely people can take.

Begin by *taking care of your physical needs.* Paul wrote to Timothy, "When you come, bring the cloak that I left with Carpus at Troas" (2 Timothy 4:13). The Roman prison cell was probably damp and cold. Paul needed the cloak to help him maintain his health and continue his writing ministry. He wanted to make the best of his bad situation. So he asked Timothy to bring his cloak.

Lonely people often fail to take care of themselves. They don't eat right, they don't exercise, and they ignore their personal and physical needs. When you're lonely, one of the best things you can do is to begin taking better care of yourself. Fix your hair. Put on make-up. Go work out. Walk, run, or ride a bike. Get dressed in the morning, especially if you plan to go anywhere. Taking care of your physical needs will help you feel better emotionally.

Second, *make positive use of your time.* There's a temptation to waste your time away. Paul also asked Timothy to bring his scrolls and parchments when he came. Paul was saying, "Bring my Bible. Bring my sermon notes. I'll capitalize on the time with no interruptions by studying, writing, and growing." This was a great change of gears for Paul. If it weren't for his prison experiences, Paul never would have slowed down long enough for us to enjoy many of his writings that are an inspiration to us today.

If you don't make some positive use of your time, Satan will use your loneliness as fertile soil to tempt you to do all kinds of stupid things. Loneliness provides a great time for reading the Bible, prayer, and growing in your relationship with the Lord. As you grow, you're going to be more interesting to others. Then you'll have more to offer others.

The third cure for loneliness is absolutely essential. *Establish some relationships at an intimate level.* The key word here is *intimate*. Intimacy is more than just having people around us. Intimacy requires a relationship that moves below the surface to become deep and meaningful. Intimacy involves the risk of making yourself known just as you are and knowing others in return. And the reason more of us don't have relationships at this level is that intimacy is so threatening.

You ask, "Where do I find people with whom I can develop relationships at an intimate level?" You look for other people who have the same need. Paul said to Timothy, "Get Mark and bring him with you, because he is helpful to me in my ministry" (2 Timothy 4:11).

Mark was one of Paul's first traveling companions. A young man, he started on Paul and Barnabas's first missionary journey. But for some reason, he bailed out and ran home to mommy before the mission was complete (Acts 13:4, 5, 13). After that "AWOL" experience, Paul refused to give Mark a second chance (Acts 15:36-40). But now, Paul himself was lonely. Maybe he got to thinking about how lonely Mark must have felt when Paul refused to allow him to serve on the second journey, so he told Timothy, "Bring him with you. He is helpful to me."

Some people think the way to remedy their loneliness is to find somebody who is sharp, popular, and who can boost their ego; then they beg for that person's attention. What they really need is to find somebody else who is lonely and reach out to them. You don't need to find somebody to love you near as much as you need to find someone you can love.

If you want to find intimacy, find other people who have the same need and love them.

She sat alone in an old people's home
Lonely and old and gray;
She wished that someone, just anyone,
Would call on her that day.
Did you?

He lay for days on his hospital bed—
The hours were long and hard.
He wished that someone, just anyone
Would send him a cheery card.
Did you?

He was far from home on foreign soil
Feeling homesick, lonely, and blue.
He wish that someone, just anyone,
Would write him a letter or two.
Did you?

Her loved one had died a few weeks ago,
So sad and heartbroken she sat;
She wished that someone just anyone,
Would come to her house to chat.
Did you?

She spent long hours, that teacher,
Giving the best she knew;
She wished that someone, just anyone,
Would speak just a brief "thank you."
Did you?

The matter of Christian service—
We are living it day by day
When we help someone, just anyone,
As we walk along life's way.
Do you?

I can almost guarantee you that if you'll reach out to
lonely people, you won't be lonely anymore. If you're

already doing that and still not finding intimacy, I would suggest you *examine your attitude.* The problem may be you.

I hear people generalize sometimes, "Everybody in this city is cold. Everybody in this church is unfriendly. Everybody in this school is a snob." No doubt, some of them—many of them—are, but many of them are very compassionate and open, too. In any large group of people, there will be somebody you can relate to if you determine to find one.

If over the course of a long period of time you have no intimate relationships, ask a trusted friend or counselor, "Why don't people want to be around me? Please be honest." Then listen and learn.

Another key to finding intimate relationships is this: be sure to *give your friends some space.* Some people are so hungry for intimacy that they scare people off by being domineering and smothering. A man who had never attended our singles group before came to one of their Bible studies and announced, "If any of you women are looking for a husband, I'm looking for a wife. Just see me afterwards." He didn't have many takers! He looked normal enough, and had a pleasant personality, but that attitude is going to drive people away.

There are some people who, if they are shown the littlest attention, become leaches. They take advantage of you. They want constant attention. And they want intimacy all the time. Your Christian friends are to be your brothers and sisters, just like in a family. That means they will try to meet needs, but they are not going to respond to your every little whim and desire.

So give people some space and respect for their privacy. They'll enjoy time with you rather than avoid time with you.

The final cure for loneliness that Paul demonstrates for us is *draw close to the Lord.* He says:

But the Lord stood at my side and gave me strength. . . . The Lord will rescue me from every evil attack and will bring me safely to his heavenly kingdom (2 Timothy 4:17, 18).

51

Where is God when you're lonely? Right next to you. Do you remember the song that says, "When you walk through a storm hold your head up high." It concludes by saying, "You'll never walk alone." If you have fellowship with God through a personal relationship with Jesus Christ, you'll never walk alone. The Bible says, "There is a friend who sticks closer than a brother"—and that friend is Jesus Christ.

Many people are lonely because of a lack of intimate human relationships, but others are lonely because of their lack of a relationship with God. Both are necessary. Both are needed. Some of you have intimate relationships with people, but you're still lonely and you can't understand why. The reason is there's a vacuum in your life that only the Son of God can fill.

As Paul faced his final days in prison, he knew he was not alone. And when the guard came to his cell and unlocked the door and said to Paul, "It's time," Paul knew he was walking out of that cell for the last time. But he wasn't by himself. Jesus Christ was with him.

I know what it's like to be alone—for Christmas, for birthdays, for days at a time! I know what it's like to wonder whether those times alone would ever end. But I have also experienced the presence of Christ in those moments—and his peace that passes understanding. I came to realize that, while I was alone, I didn't have to be lonely. There's a difference. I knew Christ was with me. As for me, I'm totally convinced that I'll never walk alone.

Questions for Discussion

1. "Ours is a society filled with lonely people," says the author (page 41). Do you agree? If so, why do you think this is true? Has it always been this way, or what makes today's situation different from the past?

2. The author lists three "surprises of loneliness": that it strikes people who are surrounded by other people, that it strikes successful people, and that it strikes Christian people. Which of these do you find most surprising? Why?

3. If Christians are lonely, does that suggest a breakdown of the proper function of the church? Why or why not? What can we do about the fact that some of our Christian brothers and sisters are lonely?

4. What can we do to lessen the loneliness of separation? In what ways would you respond differently to someone whose loneliness is caused by opposition or desertion?

5. Why do people try false cures for loneliness—workaholism, materialism, escapism, and pity parties? Do people really think these things will work, or do they do these things unconsciously?

6. Is it fair to assume every workaholic or every materialistic person is lonely? Why or why not?

7. Why is it important to take care of your physical needs when you are lonely?

8. It is possible to be alone and yet not be lonely. How can you tell if a person who is alone is also lonely and needs someone to help?

9. What can the church as a body do to be more sensitive to the loneliness of people in the church?

10. What should you do if you know someone is lonely?

CHAPTER FOUR

Healing the Hurt of Harbored Hatred

Matthew 6:12-15

Who has hurt you the most in your lifetime?

My guess is that instantly somebody just came to your mind. Very likely, it's someone who is—or, more likely, *was*—very close to you: an ex-spouse, a husband, a wife, a business partner, a parent, a son or daughter, the employer that fired you, a neighbor, an in-law, an ex-boyfriend or girl-friend.

Even the thought of that person still makes you tense up. Our minds are very adept at holding on to hurts. It's amazing how well we can hold on to things that happened months—even years—ago. The problem is that when you hold on to a hurt, it turns into hate.

We all know that occasionally people are going to hurt us. Sometimes it's by accident and sometimes it's deliberate. But hurts will come. Hurts *have* come. And some of those hurts have taken root and are growing into harbored ha-treds—hatreds we can't let go of.

One of the most important skills we can learn is to destroy our harbored hatred before our harbored hatred destroys us.

Our typical reaction when someone hurts us is to hurt him back, retaliate, and get revenge. We don't get mad; we get even. Revenge is part of the American way of life.

A guy was driving down the street one day and saw a beautiful Mercedes Benz sitting in a yard with a "for sale" sign on it. He had always wanted a Mercedes, so he stopped to inquire about it. This one was only a couple of years old and in great condition, so he began to think he was just wasting his time—he would never be able afford it. But since he had stopped, he asked the price anyway. To his surprise, the woman of the house said all she wanted was $100. Without hesitating he whipped out his check book, wrote a check, and purchased the car.

As he stuck the title in his pocket, he asked her, "I've just got to ask, why are you selling this so cheaply?"

She said, "Well, several days ago my husband ran off with his secretary. He just wired me from Hawaii and told me that I must sell this car and send him the check."

We love to get revenge like that! There's only one problem. It doesn't work. Revenge never releases our harbored hatreds. Usually, it only makes it go deeper.

▬▬▬▬▬▬▬▬▬▬▬

The High Cost of Harbored Hatred

Please understand that harbored hatred never hurts the other person. It only hurts you. Harbored hatred is always far more damaging to the person carrying it than to the object of it. Job 5:2 says, "Resentment kills a fool."

Why would the Bible refer to people who carry resentment as fools? Because no matter how much hate you have, you're never going to change what's happened. It's not going to do any good. Hate doesn't change the past. Resentment kills us, hurts us, and damages us. Resentment kills everyone foolish enough to carry it.

We don't seem to understand that resentment and revenge are a boomerang that always comes back and hurts us more than the other person. While we're stewing, the person who hurt us is oblivious to our emotions. They're out having a good time. Job 18:4 says, "You. . . tear yourself to pieces in your anger." In other words, you're the one paying the price.

There is a high cost to harbored hatred. *It costs us physically.* Harbored hatred leads to health problems, ulcers, high blood pressure, and a loss of energy. A man told his doctor, "I need more medication for my colitis."

The doctor asked, "Who are you colliding with now?"

We say things like, "He's a pain in the neck." "She's a pain in my side." "He gives me a headache." Harbored hatred really does affect us physically in those ways.

It costs us emotionally. Hate is a destructive disease in our minds. I was at a college trustees meeting when, in the course of the discussion, a person's name was brought up. All of the sudden, one of the men at the meeting rifled off three or four derogatory comments about the individual. That really caught me by surprise. Bitterness just spewed out in his words and the tone of his voice. Maybe he had a right to be angry at the person; I don't know. But I thought to myself, "If he doesn't deal with the resentment, it is going to destroy him emotionally."

In his book *None of These Diseases* (©1984, Revell), S.I. McMillen talks about the affect of resentment on our bodies. He says, "It's not what you eat, but what eats you." Depression is often brought on by our hatred. Depression is simply a depletion of emotional energy, and nothing depletes your emotional energy faster than hatred. If you're depressed and can't figure out why, the first question you should ask is, "Against whom do I have a grudge?"

Harbored hatred costs us personally. It's ironic, but any psychologist will tell you that we tend to become like the people we despise. A boy grows up hating his abusive father. He says, "I'll never be like my dad." But when he's all grown up, people look at him and say, "He's just like his dad." His resentment caused him to focus on his dad, and that's what he became.

On August 9, 1974, Richard Nixon became the first President in the history of the United States to resign from office. Having fallen from the highest position of power in the modern world, the former President said in his personal farewell address to his staff: "Those who hate you don't win until you hate them back, and that will destroy you." Richard Nixon discovered the high cost of harbored hatred. He knew, didn't he? It will destroy you. It will cost you personally.

However, the highest cost of harbored hated is what *it costs us spiritually*. Jesus summed it up this way:

> For if you forgive men when they sin against you, your heavenly Father will also forgive you. But if you do not forgive men their sins, your Father will not forgive your sins (Matthew 6:14, 15).

The cost of harbored hatred is pretty high. Too high to hold on to. If we don't forgive other people their sins against us, God's not going to forgive our sins against him. We will never be able to receive what we are unwilling to give.

We often pray in the Lord's prayer the words, "Forgive us our debts, as we also have forgiven our debtors" (Matthew 6:12). We actually are saying, "Lord, forgive me for my sins against you in the same way that I've been forgiving those who've sinned against me."

Now here's the big question: Have you forgiven those who've sinned against you? Have you forgotten it? Have you let it go? If you have, then you're in good shape. When you ask God for his forgiveness, he is going to forgive you in the same way. But if you've been struggling with harbored hatred, if you're not letting go, your heavenly Father can't forgive you for your sins. Forgiveness is a two-way street.

Somebody said to John Wesley one time, "I could never forgive that person. Never!"

And Wesley said, "Then I hope you never sin."

I know someone reading this book right now is saying, "You've got to be kidding! Forgive them after the way they've hurt me? Why should I forgive that person?" Because if you don't, it's going to cost you physically, emotionally, personally, and spiritually. It's going to eat you up. "Resentment kills a fool."

The Path to Healing Harbored Hatred

The good news is, hatred doesn't have to exact this heavy price on you. The path to healing is relatively short. You need to take just four steps.

1: Accept God's Forgiveness

If hatred is eating you up, the place to begin is to accept God's forgiveness of you. What did Jesus mean when he taught us to pray, "Forgive us our debts?" What is a *debt*? A debt is an obligation that we have to pay, something we owe.

The obligation we owe God is for our sin debts. There is a moral audit of our lives going on continually. Whenever we sin, there are ledger books in Heaven that get marked. Now our problem is, we have no means of repaying that sin debt. Contrary to popular belief, good works do not cancel out sin debts. There's nothing we can do to wipe our sin debts off the ledger. We can't knock on enough doors. We can't pass out enough literature. We can't light enough candles to eliminate our sin debts. The Bible is very clear that works can't save us.

So on the day of judgment, we're going to stand before a perfect God who has no sin debts. Everybody who shows some sin debt on the ledger will be sent to Hell. And only those who have no sin debts on their ledger are going to go to Heaven.

If you have a debt that you can't pay, somebody has to absorb the loss. Maybe you have a rich uncle who bails you out. But the debt costs him. Maybe you declare bankruptcy. Then the debt is absorbed by your creditors. The creditors have to take in on the chin. They take the hit. Somebody always takes a loss.

That is just what Jesus Christ, the perfect son of God did. He absorbed a debt for you and me that we could never pay. God couldn't just wave a wand and say, "Your sins are forgiven," because there was a debt that had to be paid. So God sent his son Jesus to absorb the beating, the humiliation, the spikes, the spear, and the crown of thorns on a cross.

You may think, "Why in the world would Jesus put himself through all of that? That doesn't make any sense." Do you know why? Because he loves you. He was not obligated to do what he did, but you are so important to him that he gave his life for you. But it's up to you to accept his forgiveness, by humbly coming to him and receiving Jesus Christ and what he did for you on the cross. When you do, that forgiveness is absolutely complete. You may have committed tabloid-worthy sins, scandalous sins, awful moral-failure sins. But when God forgives you, he remembers them no more. The ledger sheets are erased. And when you stand before him on the day of judgment, there will be no sin debts listed on your ledger sheet. All your debts will have been paid for, if you accepted God's forgiveness of you.

2: Forgive the One Who Hurt You

Only when you have accepted that vertical forgiveness from God will you then be equipped to extend forgiveness horizontally to the one against whom you are harboring hatred. Healing can't come until you forgive the person, whether he wants you to or not.

Ephesians 4:32 says, "Be kind and compassionate,. . . forgiving each other, just as in Christ God forgave you." How did Christ forgive you? On the cross he cried with his arms stretched out, "Father, forgive them, for they do not know what they are doing" (Luke 23:34). Now when Jesus said those words, "Father, forgive them," who had asked for forgiveness? Nobody. He took the initiative to forgive even when they hadn't asked for it. We need to take the same kind of initiative to forgive as Christ forgave.

Refusing to forgive a person is hypocritical when we have been the recipients of so much forgiveness from God. Now if she wants to hold on to a grudge, that's her problem, but you forgive her so you can get on with your life. You're going to keep on hurting and hurting and hurting until you forgive. Forgiveness is the key. Forgiveness is the way to be set free.

One day I was talking to a woman who, six months earlier, had been hurt and betrayed by the love of her life and the father of her children. I asked her how she was doing. She acknowledged her new life as a single parent presented her with difficult circumstances, but she took me by surprise when she added, "I've never been happier." She didn't mean she was happy about the circumstances. She had discovered that, through forgiveness, she could release her hurt. She was experiencing a new freedom in her soul as a result of releasing some sinful baggage.

Now, it's very important that I explain what forgiveness is not. Forgiveness is not pretending that the event didn't happen. Forgiveness is not wishing that it didn't happen. Forgiveness is not ignoring the hurt. Forgiveness is not saying, "Forget it. It's no big deal." Forgiveness is not demanding that the other person change before you forgive him.

The Bible says we are to forgive just as in Christ, God forgave us. We have to absorb some pain, just as he absorbed pain. But forgiveness is relinquishing our right to retaliate and doing our best to restore the relationship. Forgiveness says to others, just as God says to us, "I'll pay it myself. I'll absorb the hurt in myself and let the offender go free."

That's difficult, but the word *forgive* ends with the word *give*. We have to give up our pride and our sense of justice.

One time I preached a sermon titled, "Meet a Forgiving God." The following week I received this letter, which I share with the writer's permission:

Dear Gene,

Just a few weeks after my husband and I were married, his 13-year-old daughter came to live with us. The past 12 years of coping with her moods, greed, and self-centeredness have been an ongoing strain, but the last two years have been as much a financial as emotional drain for her dad and me. We borrowed several thousand dollars to get her out of debt, only to have to pay attorney fees for her to file bankruptcy two years later. We gave her my car outright and now must make car payments on a replacement vehicle. Last month we received our gasoline credit card bill and found she had charged $140 in just 18 days. . . getting a little gas and the rest in cash, we suspect.

I have been harboring hateful feelings toward her that I didn't care to admit to myself, God, or anyone else. I've pictured calling my credit card in as lost and wishing I could see her expression the next time she came to the register and was informed the card was not valid.

We are scheduled to drive next week and see her. I've been rehearsing every scenario with delicious anticipation of finally saying something to hurt her back! Then I heard the message on "Meet a forgiving God." I learned forgiving is not forgetting the hurt, it is absorbing it. Forgiving is relinquishing the right to retaliate. Timing is everything: here we were just days from leaving on this trip and I finally had God's answer to my repeated pleas, "What am I supposed to do and say, knowing how I feel?"

If we're ever going to become godly, if we're ever going to develop the qualities of Jesus Christ in our lives, then we've got to learn to forgive just as that step-mother has learned to forgive. For your own sake, forgive those who hurt you, whether they ask or not.

3: Deal Quickly With Your Hurts

In order to prevent your hurts from developing into harbored hatred, the best practice is to deal with your hurts immediately. Ephesians 4:26 says, "Do not let the sun go do while you are still angry." In other words, deal with your hurts swiftly. If you hold on to those hurts, they become the harbored hates that will drag you down. Deal with them quickly and let go.

I heard about one husband who said, "My wife and I never go to bed angry. . . . And we haven't had any sleep now in about five weeks!"

Have you ever taken a trip and forgotten to take the garbage out before you left? When you came home, what kind of horrendous odor met you when you opened the door? It would have been so much better if the trash had been taken out immediately.

That's what happens with harbored hatreds. We think they are out of sight and won't cause a problem. But the odor is beginning to grow, even before we realize it. If you allow the odor of resentment to build, eventually everything in your entire life seems to stink. You have to take the trash out on a daily basis, and you have to deal with hurts immediately when they arise.

Now the old excuse is, "I am going to forgive them one of these days. But I'm waiting until I feel like it, and I just don't feel like it yet." The Bible teaches that we need to forgive, and do it immediately, not because we feel like it, but because we choose to. Love is a choice.

Your feelings always follow your choices. If you say, "I'm going to start being romantic with my mate when I feel like being romantic," you'll wait a long time. You must act your way into a feeling. If you want to feel forgiving toward someone, then you have to act forgiving toward that person.

The publisher of this book, Gene Wigginton, had the opportunity to visit Dr. Martin Luther King Sr. in his Atlanta office shortly after his son, Dr. Martin Luther King Jr., was assassinated. Dr. King said, "When my son was killed, it broke my heart, but I can honestly say before God I have no hate in my heart." Dr. King had learned to deal with his hurt immediately.

4: Replace the Hatred

Finally, to complete our healing, we must replace the hatred. Jesus gave us three indications of how to do that.

But I tell you who hear me: Love your enemies, do good to those who hate you, bless those who curse you, pray for those who mistreat you (Luke 6:27, 28).

First, he says, *"Love your enemies."* Instead of resenting a person, replace the hurt with love. Take the high road. Choose to act in a positive way. Loving an enemy means you meet her needs. Love is giving people what they need, not what they deserve. That's the way God loves us. He gives us what we need, not what we deserve. If we got what we deserved, we wouldn't even be here. And we are to love those who've hurt us, not because they deserve it, but because they need it.

Second, Jesus said, *"Do good to those who hate you."* One of the quickest ways to change your attitude toward somebody is to give the person a gift—buy him a book, some flowers, some candy, something. The Bible says, "Where your treasure is, there your heart is also" (Matthew 6:21). When you give a gift to someone toward whom you've harbored hatred, it begins to change your attitude, because your heart is with him.

Third, Jesus said, *"Pray for those who mistreat you."* You can't pray for them and hate them at the same time. One of those will win out over the other. Try it sometime.

Are you allowing people who hurt you five, ten, fifteen, even twenty years ago to hurt you still because of memories? Then you need to replace the hurt. You can't *resist* your feelings, you have to *replace* them. And if you'll love them, do good to them, and pray for them, you can break the hate cycle by replacing the negative feelings of resentment and hate with positive attitudes.

I sat and visited with a couple one time whose marriage had been to the brink of disaster. This woman's husband had hurt her badly. He made a bad mistake. But he repented and has changed his life. She's forgiven him. She smiled from ear to ear and said, "Forgiveness is so wonderful!"

I said, "Can I quote you on that?"

And she said, "Oh, yes. It truly is wonderful"

I looked in her eyes and saw a woman who was free from the harbored hatred that had been threatening to ruin her life. She added, "I never could have done it without the Lord."

Jesus said, "For if you forgive men when they sin against you, your heavenly Father will also forgive you" (Matthew 6:14).

So about whom are you still holding a hateful memory? Against whom are you still very bitter? A husband? A wife? A parent? A boss? A teacher? A friend? That person's brought you a lot of pain—some of it for a long time, hasn't he? Why don't you pray right now, "Lord, I've held on to this for too long, and I'm going to let it go. I'm forgiving this person, I'm releasing this person. He is not going to ruin my life anymore."

Then pray, "Lord, replace the pain in my life with your peace. Replace the hurt in my life with your healing. Replace the bitterness in my life with your love."

He will.

And it will set you free!

Questions for Discussion

1. Why is it that "revenge is part of the American way of life"? Can you think of anyone who really got satisfaction from taking revenge? What does taking revenge do to one's spirit?
2. Job 5:2 links resentment with envy. How are they related? Why are both dangerous?

3. In what ways does harbored hatred cost a person physically? Emotionally? Personally? Spiritually? Who can afford it?

4. The author says the first step to releasing harbored hatred is to accept God's forgiveness. Why is it important to realize you yourself need forgiveness in order to forgive others?

5. The second step is to forgive the person who hurt you. Why is that so difficult? Why, if we really appreciate that Christ has forgiven us, should we forgive?

6. When someone apologizes, it is common to respond, "That's okay," or, "Forget it," or, "It's no big deal." Yet the author says that is *not* forgiveness (page 61). Are these responses inappropriate? Why or why not? If so, what would be a proper response?

7. What if the person you want to forgive will not acknowledge having done any wrong to have any need for forgiveness? How does one forgive in such a case? Why is it, perhaps, even more important to do so than when the wrong is admitted?

8. With what can you replace hatred? How is Luke 6:27, 28 helpful in replacing hatred?

9. Have you ever prayed for someone who had hurt you, or who was continuing to hurt you? What was the result?

CHAPTER FIVE

Healing the Hurt of Family Secrets

2 Samuel 13

Theirs was a family with a steamy, sordid, sexual, sinful, secret side. What's initially surprising is that they are found in the Bible. What's especially surprising is that the father of the family was one of the greatest leaders in the Bible. But what's not so surprising is that their story is very closely related to the family secrets many American families, like yours and mine, are carrying today.

Their story brings to light an important truth—**unresolved family secrets produce even more devastating family secrets.**

A Family With Secrets

It all begins with the sexual sin of the dad, King David. While David is the most famous king in Israel's history, he also goes down as history's most notorious adulterer. His secret night with Bathsheba was the beginning of a moral slide that led to the murder of his girlfriend's husband and devastating consequences in the lives of his children. David personally found forgiveness from the Lord, but his secret sin was the start of a whole cycle of secrets in his family.

The same thing happens today. Your activity today is going to affect your children tomorrow. We see that in a dramatic way when a little baby is born with a drug addiction or with AIDS. The parent's behavior affects the health of the child. Teenagers often think if they sow their wild oats when they're young, they'll get it out of their system. But they forget that their behavior in the present is going to affect the lives of their children in the future.

The Bible says the sins of the father will be visited on the children to the third and fourth generation. That doesn't mean God is going to punish your kids. It just means that sin has a way of affecting children and grandchildren indirectly. For instance, of all adolescent drug addicts today, 70% were involved in some family sexual abuse. Of all prisoners serving time for sex related crimes, 97% were themselves victims of sexual abuse.

You see "parent problems" often produce "kid problems." And when those kids are parents themselves, another cycle of parent and kid problems often develops in the next generation.

Kids grow up and one day they meet Mr. Right or Miss Wonderful, and they overdose on infatuation. They can't imagine ever having a problem in their relationship. But over time, they discover each of them has brought secret hurts into their relationship, and the relationship begins to disintegrate. They divorce, split the kids, and remarry, thinking the problem in their first marriage was the wrong spouse.

Then they bring the same problems into the next marriage and into the blended family. The blended family is much more complicated, with three sets of children: his, hers, and theirs. The intricate complexities of the blended family just emphasize more the need to get back and deal with family secrets from our past.

These family secrets are so secret that they have never been discussed—not even inside the family, let alone outside the family. Secrets, by their very definition, suggest that there's something we're very ashamed of in our lives. That's the reason it's a secret. That's the reason we keep the hurt hidden. So we carry the shame. We don't deal with it. And eventually that secret shame is a seed that produces a cycle of dysfunctional relationships in our lives and in our families.

Who knows what psychological impact David's sin had on his children? It would be nice if we could get inside of their heads a little bit. I would speculate that, at the very least, they lost a great deal of respect for their father after his sin—just as any son or daughter would. They lost a consistent example of a godly husband and father. They lost what could have been their model for normal healthy relationships in their future. Instead, they struggled for the rest of their lives with this family secret that seemed to keep leading to a devastating cycle of other family secrets.

The impact is probably best seen in the story of Amnon and Tamar in 2 Samuel 13. Amnon was David's son. Tamar was David's daughter. But there's a problem with their relationship. Amnon falls desperately in love with his beautiful half-sister Tamar. His thoughts are consumed by his passion for her.

> Amnon became frustrated to the point of illness on account of his sister Tamar, for she was a virgin, and it seemed impossible for him to do anything to her (2 Samuel 13:2).

Amnon wanted her so badly he was sick. My sister Glenda had a crush on a boy from Iowa when she was in high school. We lived in Illinois. One time he came to see her. When he arrived, my brother Gregg, who was about ten, went right up to the guy and said, "When Glenda found out you were coming, she got so excited she threw up!" Dad took Gregg to the basement and gave him a quick lesson in social etiquette!

Amnon was so head over heals about Tamar that he got sick, too. And the more he thought about her, the more he wanted her and the more frustrated he became.

Charles Mylander writes:

> When it comes to sex, some people feel that every day is terrible, horrible, unbearable. Runaway passions rule their thinking and actions. Out-of-control sexual sins drive them down deviant back roads. They hate themselves for their practices of adultery, homosexual activity or incest—and yet they cannot stop. . . . Only another sexual episode seems to give them a brief spurt of immoral pleasure before the depressing darkness returns. They feel hopeless, helpless and misunderstood.[1]

This was Amnon.

Amnon's cousin Jonadab asked him one day why he looked so haggard every morning. Amnon confessed, "I'm in love with my half-sister Tamar."

Jonadab, it turns out, was pretty sneaky. He came up with a plan:

> "Go to bed and pretend to be ill," Jonadab said. "When your father comes to see you, say to him, 'I would like my sister Tamar to come and give me something to eat. Let her prepare the food in my sight so I may watch her and then eat it from her hand'" (2 Samuel 13:5).

The plan sounded like a winner. He faked an illness. He asked his father to send Tamar to feed him. And Tamar made bread in his presence—but he refused to eat.

> Then Amnon said to Tamar, "Bring the food here into my bedroom so I may eat from your hand." And Tamar took the bread she had prepared and brought it to her brother Amnon in his bedroom. But when she took it to him to eat, he grabbed her and said, "Come to bed with me, my sister."

"Don't, my brother!" she said to him. "Don't force me. Such a thing should not be done in Israel! Don't do this wicked thing. What about me? Where could I get rid of my disgrace?" (2 Samuel 13:10-13).

This family that already had so much shame in its past was about to add one more secret to the growing list.

But he refused to listen to her, and since he was stronger than she, he raped her (2 Samuel 13:14).

Amnon did more than rape his sister physically. Rape is always more than a physical act. He raped her emotionally. He raped her relationally. He raped her spiritually.

Immediately, this brother who had to have her moments before didn't want anything to do with her, and he left her abandoned.

Then Amnon hated her with intense hatred. In fact, he hated her more than he had loved her. Amnon said to her, "Get up and get out!" (2 Samuel 13:15).

Later, when Tamar's brother Absalom discovered what had happened, he gave the typical insensitive response that many give to a victim of rape or incest. "Don't take this thing to heart" he said (2 Samuel 13:20). "Just forget about it. Put it behind you." But a memory like that is not so easily forgotten. People say, "Forgive and forget," as if we can develop a case of holy amnesia or something.

This is the last sad footnote we find in Scripture about Tamar's life:

And Tamar lived in her brother Absalom's house, a desolate woman (2 Samuel 13:20).

This family secret left a terrible scar. Tamar knew it would. She cried, "Where could I get rid of my disgrace?" She was saying, "Where could I get rid of my shame?"

I've discovered that many, many people are carrying a shame like that in their lives today, and it's adversely affecting every other relationship they have. Their current relationships are continually being ruined because they react to family secrets from the past instead of simply to the people with whom they are trying to build relationships.

I wonder how many marriages are ruined because of an unresolved family secret that involved a parent or other relative? The anger is refocused on the spouse.

Relationships in David's family got worse before they got better. This secret impacted all the other members of the family. One family member's sin always affects the others. This is typical of how co-dependency works in families where there are secret alcohol and drug addictions. An entire family is controlled by the problem of one person.

Just look at some of the devastating things that continued to happen as a result of these unresolved family secrets:

Family Relationships Break Down

> When King David heard all this, he was furious. Absalom never said a word to Amnon, either good or bad; he hated Amnon because he had disgraced his sister Tamar (2 Samuel 13:21, 22).

Often the other family members don't even recognize how the secret sin of one in the family is tearing down their own relationships. It's a secret, so they can't get help. They don't want anybody to know about dad's problem or mom's problem or brother's or sister's problem, which only makes matters worse.

A friend told me once how the moral failure of his two older married brothers has adversely affected him for years. His brothers were known as outstanding Christian family men, but both made the same mistake David did. For years, this younger brother has lived in embarrassment, fear, and shame. He has lacked confidence in his own abilities, and it's held him back, paralyzing him from doing many things he would have attempted otherwise.

Don't think for a moment that your sin isn't going to hurt anybody else. Sin always affects other family members.

Anger Turns to Hatred

Absalom's anger boiled to the point that he arranged for his brother's murder. I think that might have been prevented if David had got involved and said, "Let's face our secrets. Let's deal with these issues. Let's put them on the table. I'll talk about mine. You talk about yours." But instead, he ignored the secret and let his sons fight it out.

After Absalom had Amnon murdered, he fled the country to live with his grandfather. There he sought a father figure and a relationship he hadn't been able to find with his own dad. David was left mourning Amnon's death and the absence of Absalom.

Two years later, Absalom returned. They had another chance to deal with these family secrets. But, as usual, no issues were dealt with. Everything was swept under the carpet. They continued to carry the secrets. Absalom developed a rebellious spirit and later led a revolution against his father.

The Secret Sin Is Repeated

This family was so messed up that in the middle of the revolt, when Absalom temporarily took over Jerusalem, out in public where people could see what was going on, Absalom slept with some of his father's wives (2 Samuel 16:22).

Isn't it interesting that the same man who was incensed by his brother's incest with his sister went on to commit incest with his father's wives? We so often become the very things we hate in our family members. Unresolved family secrets just keep repeating themselves like that.

Eventually, Absalom was killed in battle. When David was informed of Absalom's death, one of the saddest scenes recorded in Scripture resulted. David stumbled up the steps of the palace sobbing, "O my son Absalom! My son, my son

Absalom! If only I had died instead of you—O Absalom, my son, my son!" (2 Samuel 18:33).

I wonder if, at that moment, David didn't wish he had intervened and dealt with their family secrets much sooner. It would have been difficult; he would have had to be honest and admit to some significant failures and sin in his life. But if he had done so, perhaps he could have helped his children to deal with their own past failures and the cycle of dysfunction could have been broken.

One thing is sure: failure to deal openly and honestly with these issues did not help!

What Are Your Secrets?

You don't have to be honest with me right now—maybe that is the reason you are reading a book on this subject instead of talking to someone. An unseen author cannot make demands on you or hold you accountable. But please be honest with yourself. What family secrets do you have that you are not dealing with today?

Maybe your family has secret *chemical addictions.*

A mother is hooked on prescription medicines.

A father is an alcoholic.

A teenager is addicted to crack cocaine.

Maybe your family is carrying secret *marriage problems.* We are all shocked when a seemingly happy marriage falls apart. But it does not happen overnight. The couple just masked the problem for a long time.

One of the most-concealed family problems is the one that kept resurfacing in David's family: secret *sexual problems.* I wish such matters did not need to be discussed, but the fact is, sexual problems are a major cause of family dysfunction today. Parents are fearful someone is going to find out about the secret of their son's homosexuality. They don't deal with the issue themselves, and it further complicates the relationship with their son.

A husband carries the secret of his adultery. He is constantly afraid his secret will be found out by his wife. In the meantime, the marriage is paralyzed until he can break out of the deception and into truth telling.

One pastor tells about a mother who walked into his office and said, "My nineteen-year-old daughter just told me that my husband has been having sexual intercourse with her since she was twelve years old." For seven agonizing years the daughter had kept the secret of her father's sexual abuse!

Please understand that families who keep sexual secrets perpetuate generations of related problems until there is an open admission and dealing with the problem.

Maybe you're dealing with secret *physical abuse.* This usually involves the abuse of women and children. Nearly six million wives will be abused by their husbands this year. Between two and four thousand will be beaten *to death!*

And physical violence is no respecter of social class. It happens in the ghetto, and it happens in the country club community. You may feel trapped by such a nightmare, fearing if you tell someone you'll experience more abuse.

Maybe your family is experiencing secret *emotional abuse.* There may not be physical or sexual abuse, but emotional abuse is destroying people from the inside out. Continual put downs, manipulation, swearing, and violent outbursts happen in what seem to be the most unlikely families. Perpetual emotional abuse can destroy a person every bit as much as physical abuse can.

I think it's important that I point out that there are many *Christians* who are carrying unresolved family secrets. David was described in the Bible as being a man after God's own heart, but still his family was messed up. Sometimes we Christians are under the mistaken impression that none of these things are ever supposed to happen to us, so we bury the secrets further. We don't want anybody to know. The reality is, these things happen in Christian families, too.

When the Nimitz freeway collapsed during the San Francisco earthquake in 1989, it was discovered that it was not the vertical supports that collapsed. It was the horizontal reinforcing steel rods that had weakened. You see, your vertical relationship with God can be right. It can be strong. But you've also got to work at having strong horizontal relationships with your family, or there may be a collapse. God's not going to let you down. It's the weak, ignored, undealt with relationships that are going to collapse.

Healing Your Family Secrets

If you are a part of a family where there are secrets and dysfunction, I want you to know there is hope. You are not trapped in an endless cycle that continues to repeat itself from generation to generation.

Sometimes we focus so much on our past environment and family record that we think we're locked into failure. We blame our parents for our own imperfections and failures. But there comes a time to grow up and go on. There comes a time for forgiveness and love. There comes a time to look forward and not backward. Some of the happiest people I know are people who overcame some horrible circumstances, and you can, too.

There's no simple 1, 2, 3 formula for surviving family secrets. I wish there were. But there are four common elements needed by those who want to find healing for their family secrets.

First, Take Ownership of the Problem

Nothing is going to be done until you do something about it. David's family kept sinking deeper and deeper because nobody was facing up to anything. There weren't any family conferences. There were no truth telling or confession sessions going on. Sometime, somewhere, somebody has to take ownership of the problem and say, "Enough is enough! We're going to take some action!" Otherwise, the unresolved family secrets will keep producing even more devastating family secrets.

I once heard about a yacht that was sitting at anchor in the Niagara River, but in a strong wind the rope broke. Unable to fight the current, the boat drifted closer and closer toward the Niagara Falls. The people in the boat panicked, accusing each other and blaming each other, while the sound of the thundering falls drew nearer. Finally, the quick thinking skipper blew a hole in the bottom of the boat with dynamite. The boat immediately began to sink in the shallow water, lodging itself on the bottom of the river, and all of the people were rescued.

That's what's going to have to happen in some of our families. You can blame others all you want, but one of these days, somebody is going to have to blow everything loose, somebody who's not afraid of an explosion, somebody who will take ownership of the problem. And, friend, that somebody is going to have to be you, or it may never happen.

Second, Tell Someone of the Problem

A second element needed for surviving your family secrets is to tell someone there's a problem. Tamar left Amnon's presence weeping loudly. Her brother Absalom discovered what had happened. Even though he didn't offer her the best advice, it was still a good move to share the problem with someone. Many of our family secrets are so complicated that we'll never come out of them unless others know.

Now, please don't misunderstand. I am not suggesting you tell anybody and everybody. Be very selective about whom you tell. But this is usually a needed step in working through family secrets.

If someone is abusing you in any way—sexually, physically, emotionally—you have the right to tell somebody what's happening. If the first person you confide in doesn't believe you, find someone who will. Keep telling until someone believes you and gets you the necessary help. That may mean telling a trusted friend, a pastor, a counselor, the police, or some kind of hot line. In families where incest is taking place, someone *must* blow the whistle.

Elizabeth Wainwright was a victim of incest. She writes,

> For any healing to come to an incestuous family, the secret must be broken, no matter how much it hurts. In our family, I was the one who had to take the responsibility of breaking the harmful silence, to risk opening up old wounds—more than once—in order to bring healing to my family.[2]

If you are in an abusive relationship, don't be naïve and believe you can handle the problem alone. Don't think you should keep the secret. It's been kept too long. Don't trust the promise of the abuser, "I'll never do it again." Victims and abusers must receive help.

And if there is an abuser reading this, I want to plead with you, tell someone! Get help before someone tells on you.

If there's drug dependency in your family, tell someone. If there's physical abuse, tell someone. Don't ever, ever put your life in danger. Get out if you have to. If there's inappropriate sexual behavior, tell someone. Help is available.

James 5:16 says, "Therefore confess your sins to each other and pray for each other so that you may be healed."

Third, Release Your Undeserved Guilt

People carrying family secrets many times heap guilt on their own shoulders that is undeserved. They blame themselves for another person's problem. This is a symptom of co-dependency.

As Amnon attempted to rape Tamar, she cried, "Where could I get rid of my disgrace?" That's the typical response of a victim of abuse. But why should Tamar be disgraced? This was not Tamar's choice. She didn't want this. Yet she heaped this undeserved sense of guilt on her shoulders.

Martha Janssen sums up these feelings:

> A grown woman
> realizes what she did for years
> to appease
>   and please her father.
> Even though she's been told
>   and knows in her mind
> that she had no choice
> from early childhood—
> she feels responsible
>   somehow at fault
>   or perhaps deserving.
> Weak, disgraced, ashamed,
> her only hope is—
> once she realizes and weeps,
> she can start to recognize
> it wasn't she who failed at all.
> She is the victim
> not the criminal.[3]

Maybe you're a victim who feels like a criminal. You're not a criminal! I'm not saying you should ignore your own faults, but don't heap guilt on yourself that you don't deserve. Remove yourself from the abusive situation and then, maybe with the help of others, confront the abuser.

Fourth, Remember It Is Possible to Change

The fourth element needed to survive family secrets is to remember the transforming power of Christ. "I can do everything through him who gives me strength" (Philippians 4:13).

A man was running through a cemetery one night. It was dark, and he stumbled and fell into a freshly dug grave. He tried and tried to get out, but it was too deep. He yelled for help, but no one heard him. So he finally gave up, curled up in a corner, and decided to get some sleep and wait until daylight. A short time later, another jogger came through the cemetery and did the exact same thing and fell right into the grave. It was so dark he couldn't see anything. He immediately started trying to climb out when suddenly he felt a hand on his shoulder. Then he heard a voice say, "You can't get out of here!" But he did.

You might think you'll never find healing for your family secrets, but through Jesus Christ you can. Even though we've had imperfect earthly parents, we are loved by a Heavenly Father who is perfect. He has no immoral secrets. He has a perfect love. He is 100% dependable. He is consistent, the same yesterday, today, and forever. And his love is available to you right now through Jesus Christ.

Are you an abusive husband, wife, or parent? An alcoholic or drug dependent person? Someone who's inflicted the silent sin of incest? Or someone enslaved to pornography, and it's controlling your life? Maybe you've been unfaithful to your marriage vows. The good news is, you can change. We need to be saying to ourselves, "I can change through Christ who gives me the strength. I can break the cycle of abuse. I can stop the habit that enslaves. I can forgive that sin that seems unforgivable. I can be forgiven by God. I can change through Christ!" Christianity is not a panacea of quick fixes, but with the power of Christ you can change, if you have the "want to."

Most family secrets have been present for far too long. Some have prayed and hoped that they would go away, but there's no magic cure. You have to face the problem head on and do something. Ask God for courage so the cycle can be broken and the same problems won't continue to be repeated.

Questions for Discussion

1. Do you agree with the author that "unresolved family secrets produce even more devastating family secrets"? Why or why not?

2. What if the family secret cannot be resolved—that is, the situation that causes shame cannot be corrected by those who are embarrassed by it? What can or should they do?
3. If you see symptoms of a secret sin—a friend's family relationships are breaking down and anger seems to be common among the family members—how far can you go as a friend and Christian brother or sister to try to help? If it is a "secret" sin, do you have a right to ask about it? Do you dare ignore it? What should you do?
4. The author lists several family secrets: chemical addictions, marriage problems, sexual problems, and physical, or emotional abuse. What are some other problems people try to keep secret?
5. Why is it so hard to admit to a situation that is not your fault—such as being abused? Why is it so important to do so?
6. These things are kept secret because they are embarrassing. How does one get up the nerve to come out of the closet and admit to a secret sin? How can a loving Christian fellowship help people gain such courage? Would people in *your* church feel safe in admitting a secret sin? Why or why not?
7. Why is it important to realize some guilt we feel is undeserved? What can we do about such feelings?
8. What about guilt that is deserved? How should we deal with that? How can Philippians 4:13 give us courage to deal with it?

---

[1]Charles Mylander, *Running the Red Lights*, © 1986, Regal Books, Ventura, CA.

[2]Elizabeth Wainright, "Can You Ever Forgive Incest?" *Family life Today*, May, 1984, p. 38.

[3]Reprinted from *Silent Scream*, by Martha Janssen, ©1983, Fortress Press. Used by permission of Augsburg Fortress.

CHAPTER SIX

Healing the Hurt of Continuing Grief

1 Kings 17:17-24

One morning shortly after my father died at the premature age of 52, my brother Gregg, my Mom, and I were about to eat breakfast out on the patio. Mom gave Gregg the plates to go set the table. A moment later, he returned with a pained look on his face. She had given him one too many plates. Mom wept.

Grieving is painful.

As Christians, we look forward to a reunion in Heaven, but in the meantime, our separation from loved ones hurts. In the meantime, we sorrow, we mourn, we grieve.

Grief is the emotion we experience whenever we lose something valuable to us. We grieve when we lose people, when we lose possessions, and when we lose position. You can grieve when you lose your job or when you're forced to retire. We grieve when we move from one city, leaving behind memories, relationships, and a home, to move to another. We grieve when a boyfriend or girlfriend dumps us.

We grieve over the breakup of a marriage. Parents grieve when a son or daughter heads down a path of self-destruction. Have you ever talked to a couple who desperately would like to have children, and have not been able to yet? They grieve.

I am able to do only a limited amount of counseling. Still, it's enough that one day I realized that almost all of the issues people are dealing with are related to grief in one form or another. So I think this subject has application to all of us who have ever lost anything of value.

Some are under the mistaken impression that Christians aren't supposed to grieve. They think grieving is a sign of spiritual weakness. But the Bible never says that. First Thessalonians 4:13 says we are not to grieve "as those who have no hope," but it doesn't say not to grieve. It just says we are not to grieve in the same, hopeless way as non-Christians.

Jesus grieved. The prophet Isaiah called him a "man of sorrows" (Isaiah 53:3). When Lazarus died, Jesus was troubled and deeply moved. He wept with the other mourners, even though he knew he was going to raise Lazarus from the dead. In the Garden of Gethsemane Jesus was deeply grieved.

Maybe you're grieving right now. You've experienced a miscarriage—death before birth. You work with the terminally ill, and you grieve over each patient you lose. You are dealing with the loss of a child, a parent, a husband, a wife, or a very special friend.

There is a story in 1 Kings 17 about a woman who was also in grief. She was a widow from a town called Zarephath. She had grieved the death of her husband some time before. She had to adjust to being a single mother, trying to be both the father and mother to her son. She had gone through the difficult adjustments of losing the one who had provided for all of her physical needs. Obviously, her husband didn't have any life insurance; there was no pension to collect. His death had left her in a position of poverty.

However, into this widow's life God brought a prophet named Elijah. She didn't have anything to give him, but she was faithful to taking care of this special servant of God as much as she was able. God honored her faithfulness by miraculously refilling her jar of flour and jug of oil so she could make bread for them to eat every day.

Everything seemed to be going so well—for a while. This widow, living in the heart of a pagan land, began to take notice of the God Elijah followed. Then, one day, everything came crashing in.

A Difficult Death to Grieve

Some time later the son of the woman who owned the house became ill. He grew worse and worse, and finally stopped breathing (1 Kings 17:17).

The Living Bible says simply, "The woman's son became sick and died." This death was especially difficult because it involved a child. There's no harder funeral to conduct or attend than that of a child. The first funeral I can ever remember attending was when I was very young. A boy had been accidentally killed while playing with a gun. I don't remember a lot, but I do remember the tears and agony in the eyes of everyone, especially the parents.

The circumstances around some deaths naturally make the normal grieving process more difficult or complicated. That's true *with an extremely untimely death*—not only the death of a child, but the death of a teenager, or an adult who is in the prime of life. The fact that this woman had already lost her husband was bound to make her grieving process even more difficult.

Since this widow had a young son, it's likely that her husband had died an untimely death. He was probably young, in the prime of his life. I recently conducted the funeral of my ninety-three-year-old Grandma Crooks. We grieved, but it's a little different kind of grief because we expected it. Grief is usually more difficult *when a tragic mode of death is involved*: a car accident, a suicide, a murder.

Grief is more complicated *when you feel a responsibility in the death*. Maybe you were the driver of a car involved in a fatal accident. Maybe you feel guilty that you didn't help your loved one watch his diet better and encourage him to exercise more.

Grieving can be more difficult *when you were close to the deceased*. It may be that now you have no other close relationships. Or maybe you were extremely dependent on that person to give you your sense of identity, self-confidence, and meaning in life. After my dad died, one day my mom came across a book that dad had given her years earlier. He had inscribed on the inside jacket, "To my sweet wife, who makes me a better man, and our home a paradise." When you lose that kind of affirmation, you lose something special.

Grieving can be more complicated *when you have made promises* to the person who has died, and they are difficult to keep. You feel guilty. Maybe she made you promise you wouldn't grieve or be sad, so you try to hold in your emotions. Maybe he made you promise you wouldn't remarry, or move, or so on.

Grieving is more complicated *when you prematurely resume all of your normal activities* and routines. The reality of the death is never really acknowledged.

Signs of Normal Grief

This mother in our text was angry. She was bitter. She said to Elijah, "What do you have against me, man of God?" (1 Kings 17:18).

It's easy to understand why she was bitter. Everything had been going so well. She was finally getting over her husband's death. She had witnessed God's daily replenishing of the oil and flour. But just about the time she was gaining confidence in God and rebuilding her life, everything fell apart. She must have wondered, "If God were really taking care of my daily needs, how could he have let this happen?"

She did what many of us have done, she became embittered at God. She blamed God and blamed the preacher Elijah, who represented God. She even began to believe she was being punished by God for her sin. She said to Elijah, "Did you come to remind me of my sin and kill my son?" (1 Kings 17:18).

This is a common misconception today: "if you suffer tragedy, God must be displeased with you and is punishing you." Many times we do reap what we sow, but please note this: most pain is not directly associated with our sin. The fact that this child died had nothing to do with whether this widow was walking in the will of God or not. It had everything to do with the fact that the boy lived in a fallen world where there are germs, sickness, viruses, and diseases.

Those who've studied the grieving process will tell you that these reactions by this mother are very normal. Bitterness, blaming God, and blaming oneself are all emotions most people go through in the normal grieving process. Let me try to show you some of the normal stages of grief by summing them up in three steps.

Initial Reactions

Grief usually begins with an emotional shock. You just can't believe the person is gone. Sometimes when you see someone at a funeral you say, "Oh she is doing so well; she is at such peace." But she may well not be at peace. She is more likely still in a state of shock. It's common in these early stages of grief to experience numbness, denial (This can't be happening. I keep thinking he'll walk through that door.), bitterness (like the widow), intense crying, and even an emotional collapse. These are all normal and healthy signs of grief in its initial stage. Remember tears are a very important release of tension that we need to let flow in this stage.

Enduring Grief Symptoms

This second step is the most difficult. Most people seem to think you are done with grieving when you get through the initial reaction, so you have little or no support. People who carried in meals, sent cards, and checked on you now seem to think everything is normal now, but it's not.

You experience times of sorrow that can drag on for months. One day you're restless, another day depressed, another day apathetic, another day overcome with memories, another day overwhelmed by loneliness. The simplest activities that used to be done automatically now require great effort and the expenditure of considerable energy. You may experience trouble sleeping, exhaustion, weakness, headaches, shortness of breath, indigestion, loss or an increase of appetite, anxiety, forgetfulness, a declining interest in sex, and dreams about the deceased.

Special days are especially difficult through the first year—the first Christmas, the first Easter, the first birthday, the first anniversary without them. C. S. Lewis described this step of his own grief this way,

> Tonight all the hells of young grief have opened again, the mad words, the bitter resentment, the fluttering in the stomach, the nightmare unreality, the wallowed-in-tears. For in grief nothing "stays put." One keeps on emerging from a phase, but it recurs. Round and round. Everything repeats. Am I going in circles, or dare I hope I am on a spiral? But if a spiral, am I going up or down it?

Thankfully this stage doesn't last forever.

Re-emerging Into Life

Slowly, painfully, reluctantly, experimentally, the person in grief re-emerges back to living. Life is not the same. There have been many changes. But it does resume. And it is worthwhile. You recognize that the sun is still shining;

you just couldn't see it because of the clouds. But gradually you are climbing above the clouds to see hope again.

The widow in Zarephath had resumed her life after the death of her husband because there was a son who needed her. If you ever want to get through your loss, you must open yourself to new and different human relationships. I know you want to run away from life. The last thing you want is to try something new. You can think of a thousand different reasons why you'd rather stay home and be gloomy than go out and be forced to be nice to people and think new thoughts. However, that's only going to prolong your grief.

If you've lost your physical and emotional support system, you're going to have to establish new ones. My mom and dad always did a lot of entertaining. When a couple came to our house, Mom and Dad would always have a hug for both the husband and the wife. But when mom was left alone, that became awkward. She didn't feel comfortable with those same friendly gestures anymore. She realized she would have to make new friends. So she started a support group and Bible study for other women in grief. It helped a number of the other women, but most of all it helped Mom because she needed them. It was a new network of relationships. They could lend emotional support to one another.

Re-emerging involves changes in responsibility. My dad used to get after my mom because she never checked the gas gauge on her car. Well, she didn't have to. Dad always took care of it. Shortly after he died, guess what? Mom ran out of gas one day. But it only happened one time. You learn to take on new responsibilities when you re-emerge.

You may be asking, "How long does it take to go through these steps and re-emerge?" It's different for everybody, but most specialists agree that the most intense portion of grieving should be completed within a year or two. If it continues longer, it's a pretty good indication that there is unhealthy continuing grief going on. For some reason the normal stages of grief didn't happen. This person has got stuck somewhere.

―――――――

Signs of Unhealthy Continuing Grief

If someone you know has been grieving the death of a loved one for two years or more, I would get concerned about that person. Be especially attentive. If you see one or more of these warning lights, consider getting the person some help.

1. I would be concerned if your friend is under the increasing conviction that he or she is no longer valuable as a person.
2. I would be concerned if you witness self-destructive threats or behavior.
3. I would get concerned if your friend is still completely withdrawing from others and refusing to interact.
4. I would be concerned if the person seems to be coping with grief by excessive drinking or drug use.
5. I would be concerned if he seems to be preoccupied with the dead person. Sometimes people will venerate objects that remind them of the deceased or link them to the deceased. Another unhealthy sign is the refusal to change the deceased person's room. All of her clothing and possessions are exactly where she left them.
6. I would be concerned about extreme emotional expressions, or resistance to any offers for help or counseling.
7. I would be concerned if the griever has never let the death emotionally affect him. That usually indicates long-term denial or grief avoidance.

Obviously, some of these behaviors are dangerous no matter how long it has been since the death of the loved one. Items 1, 2, and 4 should be cause for concern and corrective action any time they are displayed. But the others are somewhat normal at first. It is only when they continue that they may signal a problem.

In 1 Samuel 16:1 the Lord said to Samuel, "How long will you mourn for Saul, since I have rejected him as king over Israel? Fill your horn with oil and be on your way." There comes a point where we are stuck and the Lord says, "It's time to move on. Get back into life. Establish new routines. Be on your way. You've been in mourning long enough."

That doesn't happen right away. There's always a time of waiting when you're grieving the loss of a loved one. But there comes a time to get back into life. There comes a time when the worst of the grieving should be over and life should resume.

Healing for Continuing Grief

I want to give four remedies, based on Scripture, for finding healing for continuing grief.

First, Let Others Help

When the widow's son died, Elijah said to her,

> "Give me your son," . . . He took him from her arms, carried him to the upper room where he was staying, and laid him on his bed (1 Kings 17:19).

Even after lashing out at Elijah, she let him get involved. There was probably a side of her that didn't want to let Elijah get involved. She might have been tempted to say, "I can handle this myself. You've done enough!"

Sometimes those in grief shut themselves off from other people. That is not wise. God has provided those people to help you survive. In Job 2, his friends came and just sat with him for seven days after the death of his ten children. They didn't say anything, but they were there.

My cousins Doug and Terry live in Denver. They are a couple of nuts! Three months after I had begun my ministry in Las Vegas, Doug and Terry showed up at church one Sunday morning. They entered through a side door at the front of the auditorium wearing Groucho Marx noses and glasses. They paraded across the front of the room and sat in the front row. It's amazing the elders let me stay after that!

These same cousins flew in and surprised me in a set-up at a local restaurant for my birthday a few years ago. They went so far as to get the restaurant people to let them wear their uniforms!

These same cousins love to pull unsuspecting people aside when they visit Central and say, "I've never been here before. Tell me about this preacher. I hear he's no good."

But these same cousins, with whom I love to laugh, have also been there when I needed to cry with them. These are the same cousins who got in a car and drove with their dad over a thousand miles to be with me and my family when they found out my dad had had a heart attack. I'll never forget when they got out of their car. It was another one of their surprises. It was a balm for a hurting family. I learned that week in 1974, you can't survive grief if you don't let others help.

If you're stuck in your grief, let others help. You need someone to be able to discuss your highs and lows with. You need someone to say, "Hey, think about what you just said or did. Does that make any sense?" You need someone who raises questions about your future and challenges you to make realistic plans. You need someone who will discuss practical issues like raising children, meeting financial needs, and dealing with your sexual frustrations.

Maybe you are not dealing with continuing grief, but you're around people who are. If you want to help them, you're going to have to begin accepting them where they are and not where you want them to be. Don't put unrealistic expectations on them. It doesn't do any good to tell them to snap out of it. They can only move from where they are one step at a time, and you need to walk with them through each step.

Let God Help

Elijah was grieving over the death of the widow's son, too. So he cried out to the Lord, "O Lord my God, have you brought tragedy also upon this widow I am staying with, by causing her son to die?" (1 Kings 17:20). I like how honest Elijah was with God. He had doubts, too. He prayed, "God, how could you let this happen? In the midst of all the blessings you've been bringing, why would the widow's son all of the sudden die?"

I want to encourage you not to be afraid to express your strong emotions to God like that. Tell him how you're feeling. If you're angry, if you doubt, if you hurt—*tell him!* He can take that honest plea of grief and turn it into joy. Jesus said in Matthew 5:4, "Blessed are those who mourn, for they will be comforted." God said in Jeremiah 31:13, "I will turn their mourning into gladness. I will give them comfort and joy instead of sorrow." Jesus told the disciples in John 16:20, "Your grief will turn to joy.

The Bible tells us that one of the functions of the Holy Spirit, God's presence in the believer, is to be a comforter. Some of you who've never experienced the death of a loved one wonder how others survive. They simply experience the work of the Comforter. Only when you have been through a grief experience and felt him minister to you will you know what I mean.

Be Persistent

Elijah didn't give up easily.

> Then he stretched himself out on the boy three times and cried to the Lord, "O Lord my God, let this boy's life return to him!" (1 Kings 17:21).

Elijah was persistent. He cried out to the Lord three times! The Bible teaches us to keep on seeking, keep on knocking, keep on asking. Amazingly, up to this point, there is no account anywhere in Scripture of anybody's being raised from the dead. Elijah was asking for something that he had never seen or heard of happening. He truly believed that God could bring some good out of this tragedy.

When you grieve, I want to encourage you to be persistent at working through it. Be persistent about performing your daily duties, your routines. There's a temptation to pull back, call in sick, show up late, do a sloppy job, stay in bed and complain. However, that only compounds the problem. The next day, you feel guilty and more depressed. When you're depressed, force yourself to go through the motions of your responsibilities, even when you don't want to. Eventually you'll discover that your feelings will follow your actions.

Give God the Glory for Working in Your Circumstances

God will always work in your circumstances. In this particular text, he worked in quite a miraculous way:

> The Lord heard Elijah's cry, and the boy's life returned to him, and he lived. Elijah picked up the child and carried him down from the room into the house. He gave him to his mother and said, "Look, your son is alive!" (1 Kings 17:22-24).

Notice this woman didn't give Elijah the glory. She gave God the glory: "Now I know that you are a man of God and that the word of the Lord from your mouth is the truth" (1 Kings 17:24).

Now God may not raise your loved one physically from the dead in this life, but for those who know Christ there is a promise of resurrection in the next. I think one of the greatest ways you can give God glory for helping you through your grief is to help others through theirs.

Leslie Flynn tells of a missionary couple who lost all six of their children in a monsoon flood in India. They had only been on the mission field a few months. In their grief, they wondered what they would do with all six children gone. Soon they began to gather up abandoned children on the streets of Calcutta. They started an orphanage and eventually became parents to over 300 children who never would have survived otherwise. Second Corinthians 1:4 says God "comforts us in all our troubles, so that we can comfort those in any trouble with the comfort we ourselves have received."

I don't want to be unrealistic. I don't think you ever get completely over your grief. But I want you to see you can survive it. There is healing. Revelation 21:4 says that, when we get to Heaven, God will wipe every tear from our eyes. Evidently there are some tears that we have now that won't be totally wiped away until we get to Heaven. Only God can wipe them away.

John 20 is a scene of grieving. The disciples have lost the one to whom they had entrusted their entire lives. Jesus had died on a cross. They thought their reason for living was gone. You ask, "Did they survive?" John 20:20 says, "The disciples were overjoyed when they saw the Lord."

Have you ever seen Jesus? He is the one who can turn your sadness into joy!

"Whoever believes in him shall not perish but have eternal life" (John 3:16).

Questions for Discussion

1. Have you experienced a loss that caused you grief? Were you surprised at how long it took you to stop grieving?
2. The author says, "Almost all of the issues people are dealing with [for which they see counselors] are related to grief in one form or another." Do you agree? Why is grief so common? Why is it so hard to overcome?
3. "The circumstances around some deaths naturally make the normal grieving process more difficult or complicated"

(page 85). The author lists an extremely untimely death (a child or young person), a tragic sort of death, a death for which one feels responsible, a death of someone especially close, or a death of one to whom a person has made special promises that are hard to keep. Can you think of others? What can Christians do in these cases to be able to give long-term comfort to the people grieving as a result?

4. Grief is normal. What are some actions and attitudes one might expect of a grieving person? How does understanding grief help people around a grieving person minister to the person's needs more effectively?

5. Sometimes grief goes on too long or takes a dangerously unhealthy twist. Look at the list on page 90: what should a Christian do if he sees these signs in a person? (Suggest some responses for each item.) Would you react differently to such signs in another Christian than in a non-Christian? Why or why not?

6. The author's first suggestion for healing continuing grief is to "let others help." What if the grieving person refuses your help? What should you do then?

7. The author says, "I don't think you ever get completely over your grief" (page 95). Do you agree or disagree? If you agree, does that suggest a potential ministry or support group for victims of grief?

8. Some support groups become occasions for griping instead of for growing. How can a support group for grief victims stay positive?

CHAPTER SEVEN

The Hidden Hurt of God

Every parent will tell you that bringing a child into the world and seeing him take his first steps through childhood, survive adolescence, and experience the realities of adulthood is an emotional roller coaster that produces some of life's greatest joys and many of life's most painful hurts.

We've all heard it many times—"When our first child was born was the greatest feeling in the world. To see this little bundle of life was indescribable. It was a miracle."

My parents' first three children were girls. Little did they know they were yet to get three boys! My dad was the pastor of a church that had a bell tower. He was so excited when the first boy, my brother Gregg, was born that he went down and rang the church bells so the entire town could celebrate. I'm sure it was a rather quiet celebration in most homes, but you couldn't tell my dad that. This was big news! He went to the edge of town to the sign that said, "Lincoln, IL, population 17,000," and hung a banner that said, "It's a boy!"

The Bible says, "Rejoice with those who rejoice; mourn with those who mourn" (Romans 12:15). I think most parents would say it's easiest to obey that verse when it comes to their kids. When you hear your kids say their first words, see them take their first steps, say their first prayers—you rejoice! When your little one falls down for the first time and skins her knee, when she bumps her head on the coffee table—you mourn. And that's true all her life. When you watch your kids adjust well to school, you rejoice. When you see other kids reject them and hurt your kids, you mourn.

And the older they get, the emotional extremes seem to get greater and greater. When you watch them make a courageous moral choice, do the right thing, and give their lives to Jesus Christ, you are so proud. But when you watch them make a disastrous moral choice, do the wrong thing, and cave in to peer pressure, you are so hurt.

Parenting is a very emotional experience. Just look at the hurt in the eyes of a mother when she knows her child is hurting. Sometimes it's hard to tell who hurts more, the parent or the child.

We need to understand that God is a Heavenly parent like that. We can't see God, so when he rejoices with us, his joy is hidden. And when he hurts with us, his hurt is hidden. But the fact that God's feelings are hidden from us does not make them any less real. As a parent, God is not exempt from feelings. He is not a cool iceman who watches our lives from afar without any emotional involvement. Like any parent, when you rejoice, he rejoices. When you hurt, he hurts.

In this chapter I want to explore three facts about God we seldom think about.

God Has Emotions, Too

You say, "Come on. This omniscient, omnipresent being has emotions?" He sure does!

God Experiences Compassion

In Exodus 3, the children of Israel are under oppression as slaves to the Egyptians. They have cried out to God for help. And God has *compassion* on them. God says to Moses, "I have indeed seen the misery of my people in Egypt. I have heard them crying out because of their slave drivers, and I am concerned about their suffering" (Exodus 3:7).

You can be confident that God is concerned about your suffering, too, because he is a compassionate God.

God Experiences Anger

While Moses was up on the mountain receiving the Ten Commandments, the ungrateful Israelites were down in the valley building a golden calf to worship instead of him. Moses says to the Israelites in Deuteronomy 9:7, "Never forget how you provoked the Lord your God to anger in the desert." Here's an instance where God's children ticked him off.

Do your kids ever tick you off? Of course, they do. There are moments when you can identify with the mother who was asked if she could do it all over again, would she still have children. She said, "Oh, yes! Just not the same ones."

Our Heavenly Father Experiences Jealousy

In Exodus 34:14, the Israelites were instructed, "Do not worship any other god, for the Lord, whose name is Jealous, is a jealous God."

God Even Experiences the Emotion of Hate

He says in Malachi 2:16, "I hate divorce." He hates it because it breaks a relationship that he joined together. He hates what it does to families. He hates how it hurts kids. He hates to see you suffer through the pain of divorce.

I hope you're beginning to sense that God has real emotions. He's not an uncaring, unfeeling, unemotional, cosmic ice cube. He has compassion; he gets angry and jealous. There are things he hates. And he experiences a full range of other emotions as well.

I've written about *our* hidden hurts throughout this book, but we're not the only ones suffering in secret. That is the second fact we need to consider.

God Has Hidden Hurts, Too

Just as kids do things and go through things that hurt their parents, there are things we do and go through that hurt God. Sometimes we keep things from our parents in order not to hurt them, but there's nothing that you can keep from God. Hebrews 4:13 says, "Nothing in all creation is hidden from God's sight. Everything is uncovered and laid bare before the eyes of him to whom we must give account." We cannot "spare his feelings." He knows what we do and what happens to us, and he hurts with us.

I want to identify four things in our lives that hurt God, even though his hurt is hidden from us.

God Hurts When We Fail Him

In Noah's day, the world got so bad, people were so sinful, that Genesis 6:6 says, "The Lord was *grieved* that he had made man on the earth." Notice that our sin *grieves* God; it hurts him.

We've talked about dealing with our grief in the last chapter, but God experiences grief, too. Every time we sin, it's like a little dagger piercing God's heart. He feels it just as any parent. Psalm 69:5 says, "You know my folly, O God; my guilt is not hidden from you."

To be honest, there are some things I'd rather God not know about me. Still the fact remains: God knows all about my sins and failures. I can't hide my sins from God. There are some things we can hide from our earthly parents, but there's nothing we can hide from God. Proverbs 5:21 says, "For a man's ways are in full view of the Lord, and he examines all his paths." In other words, you and I always have an audience. Nothing you ever say is off the record. Everything you think, say, do, and feel is seen by God.

We've all been in situations where we wondered:

- What if my parents find out what I've been doing?
- What if my wife—my husband—my boss—finds out?
- What if the *IRS* finds out?

No matter who it is you are worried will find out, the truth is you've already been found out! God knows, and he is grieving. And he's the only one who really counts. When you decide to come to God and confess your faults to him, he's not surprised. He's not shocked. He doesn't say, "Oh, no! How could that have happened?" Instead, he says, "I know. I saw it coming. I know why it happened. I've been sitting here grieving and waiting for you to come to me to talk about it."

If you want to take God's hurt away, the thing you need to do is to be honest with God. The Bible says, "If we say we have no sins, we deceive ourselves and the truth is not in us." So just admit, "God, I'm not fooling you. You've got my number. And I'm sorry I've hurt you. Please forgive me through the blood of Jesus Christ." You may be fooling other people. You may be fooling everyone in your family or everyone in your church, but you're not fooling God. He's got your number. He's got you pegged.

I don't know if you're like me, but it kills me to do anything that I know disappoints or hurts my mother. I don't want to hurt my mother in any way. And if you feel that way, just remember that's the same kind of hurt we bring to the heart of the Lord when we fail him. The only solution is to depend on his unconditional love, admit it to him, and ask him to forgive you. And then both of you can let it go and it's forgotten.

God Hurts When We Hurt

There's a good chance, if you've read this book, you're hurting right now. That's the reason you picked it up. So you've been reading and saying, "No one understands me. . . ." Some of you have said that to yourselves for so long that you've forgotten God understands you completely. He's watching this crisis in your life, and he's hurting with you. David wrote in Psalm 31:7, "For you [God] saw my affliction and knew the anguish of my soul."

When you experience the hurt of a broken heart, or a guilty conscience, or lingering loneliness, or harbored hatred, or family secrets, or continuing grief, your Heavenly Father hurts, too. Nobody else in this world may really know the hurt you're going through, but God knows and he's hurting right along with you, just as any parent would.

Psalm 56:8 says, "You have seen me tossing and turning through the night. You have collected all my tears and preserved them in your bottle! You have recorded every one in your book" (TLB). No hurt, no tear, goes unnoticed by God. Often hurting people feel very lonely and isolated. Maybe you've gone through a death in the family, or a divorce, or you've been fired. You feel all alone, and you think, "Nobody understands the way I feel. Nobody feels the pain."

God understands. God feels the pain. He's recording every one of your tears in his book. God feels the hurt in your heart, so why don't you respond by giving your hurts to him?

Parents know there are times when you're hurting *for* your kids. You want so badly to help them, but you can't help them until they ask you. And you think, "If only they would humble themselves and come and ask for my help." That's the way God waits for us. First Peter 5:7 says, "Cast all your anxiety on him because he cares for you."

God Hurts When We Worry

Worry is future oriented. You don't worry about the past. You may grieve over it, but worry is always over the future:

—What might happen?

—What could go wrong?

—How would I ever handle that?

God knows all about our future. He knows what your future holds. And he's going to give you the strength to deal with whatever happens in your future. That is the reason your worry hurts God. He's hurt that you don't trust him. He's hurt that you're spending yourself in worry when worry can't change the future or add a single day to your life. Psalm 139:16 says, "All the days ordained for me were written in your book before one of them came to be." Jeremiah 29:11 says, "'For I know the plans I have for you,' declares the Lord, 'plans to prosper you and not harm you, plans to give you hope and a future.'"

God *knows* the plans he has for you. God *knows* your future. All the days ordained for you were written in your biography before you were ever born.

Everybody seems to be interested in the future today. It's interesting to see what people will try in order to discover what the future holds—astrology, horoscopes, reading tea leaves, consulting with psychics, bio-rhythms, tarot cards. People try all kinds of things to find out what's going to happen next. Unfortunately, they are going to the wrong source. There *is* someone who knows what's going to happen next, but it's God. The fact is, God sees our tomorrows today. He already sees the things we'll face. I don't know about you, but that gives me great confidence in God. It's comforting to me that he knows everything that is going to happen in my life. He's already prepared for anything I'm going to face tomorrow. And the inevitable crisis that you are going to experience next month or next year—while it may catch *you* by surprise—is the crisis God has been preparing for. God never says, "Oh, I sure didn't expect that to happen!" He knows. No wonder it hurts him to see us worrying about those things now. He's going to help us when the time comes.

So what should we do with our worries? Give them to God and ask for his advice, because he knows what's going to happen. Jeremiah 33:3 says, "Call to me and I will answer you and tell you great and unsearchable things you do not know." God's not going to lay out your whole life for you and tell you everything that's going to happen. If he did, you'd get very discouraged or very full of pride. So he says, "Call to me and I'll give you advice because I know what's going to happen."

Since I live in Las Vegas, I've taken many visiting friends and family members to see Hoover Dam. In fact, I think they may give me a prize for bringing the most visitors. The roads to the dam are narrow and winding. Often I've got caught behind a car or truck and thought, "If I could just see around the curve, I'd go ahead and pass this guy." If there were a helicopter overhead that could see the whole perspective, he could radio down to me and say, "There's not another car for miles, so go ahead and pass the next three cars around the curve."

God sees what's going to happen to us around the curves in our lives, so you don't have to worry. Just ask him for advice.

If you struggle with worry, when you get up in the morning and spend some quiet time with the Lord, why don't you pray something like, "Lord, you've already seen this day that I'm about to experience. You know ahead of time every interruption I'm going to face, every cranky person, every flat tire, every traffic jam, every missed plane, every spilled cup of coffee on my suit. You've already seen it. Give me the strength to cope through this day because you know what I'm going to need."

If you're married, one day one of you is going to die first. That's almost inevitable. One of you will lose your partner first. That can be devastating. But do you know what? God already knows when and how it's going to happen. God is prepared for that event. Don't hurt him by worrying about it. He's waiting to comfort you and hold you in his arms. You can say to him now, "Lord, when it comes, give me the wisdom to know what to do. Give me the strength to know how to handle it because I know it's not going to catch you by surprise." God knows all about your futures, so you don't have to worry.

God Hurts When We Are Afraid

I think one of the biggest fears of people in the 90s is our finances, how we will provide for our needs. Jesus said in Matthew 6:8, "Your Father knows what you need before you ask him." Notice the word *knows*. God *knows* what you need.

Now if God knows everything that you need, and if he has promised to take care of our needs, how do you think it makes him feel when he sees us running around in fear about whether we're going to get by or not? Don't you think that might hurt him just a little bit? Don't you think there's a side of him that says, "Everything that person is and has is because of me. Does she really think I'm not going to take care of her basic needs if she'll just trust me?"

Do you ever act as if God is unaware of your bills? You say, "Don't you see God? I'm going under! I just can't make it." When you forget that God knows your needs, you get uptight, you get a headache, and you get upset. You fall apart and worry that your needs won't be met.

Worry is the result of not recognizing the omniscience of God. When you think God is unaware, doesn't care, doesn't see, and is totally oblivious, you begin to worry. Then you say, "Oh, I'm going to have to take control of this." Worry is trying to play God and assuming responsibility for things God never intended you to have.

But your Father knows what you need *before* you ask him. God is aware of every single need you have—financial needs, spiritual needs, relational needs, emotional needs, sexual needs, every kind of need you have in your life. And God knows those needs before you even come to him and ask him to meet them in prayer. Prayer is never giving God information that he doesn't have. God doesn't need us to check in like a reporter and say, "God, this is Gene Appel reporting in from Las Vegas to tell you what's going on in his life." He already knows what's going on in my life.

You don't pray to tell God your needs; you pray to show you're trusting him. Then he can release his blessing into your life. He's waiting for us to ask him to help while we're wrestling around trying to do it all ourselves. The Bible says, "You do not have, because you do not ask God" (James 4:2).

How should we respond when we're afraid? Just trust God. Don't panic. Pray! Don't hurt God by acting as if the God who brought the world into existence isn't capable of helping to keep a roof over your head and food on your table this month.

But there's one last fact I want you to know about God.

God Rejoices

Let me give you a couple of different ways that you can make God rejoice.

God Rejoices When You "Do the Right Thing"

Did you know that every time you do the right thing, God is watching? Matthew 6:1, 4 says, "Be careful not to do your 'acts of righteousness' before men, to be seen by them. . . . Your Father, who sees what is done in secret, will reward you." Notice every good deed will be rewarded by God. Regardless of how insignificant, regardless of whether anyone else on earth saw it or not, it will be rewarded. "God is not unjust; he will not forget your work and the love you have shown him as you have helped his people and continue to help them" (Hebrews 6:10).

•Every word of encouragement you give to others.
•Every kind word or compliment you give to your children.
•Every time you do a thoughtful act for your husband.
•Every time you pick up around the office when it's not your job.
•Every time you help out as an usher at church.

- Every act of courtesy.
- Every time you had the opportunity to be critical or gossip and you didn't.
- Every time you gave a cup of cold water in Jesus' name.
- Every time you quietly gave sacrificially to the Lord and his work.
- Every time you chose not to sin.
- Every time you took a stand for something.

God says, "I saw it all, and I will reward you."

Can't you just see God, when you do these quiet little acts that nobody else knows about, saying, "Hey, that's my boy. That's my girl. I'm proud to be their Father."

Imagine yourself the only person on a giant stage. And you're acting out your life. In the audience is only one person, God. He's out there clapping and saying, "I saw that good thing you just did. Way to go! I knew you could do it. Keep it up. Nobody else may have seen it. But I know that thought you just had was a pure, positive, good thought—and I saw it."

More and more in my life, I find myself wanting to live my life for an audience of one: God. He's all that counts. It really doesn't matter how I appear in public. What matters is how I *am* in private.

It's your character, not your reputation, that is important. Your reputation is what other people say about you. Character is what you really are. What matters is the integrity in your life when nobody is looking, because there *is* Somebody looking.

I don't know about you, but to know that God is up there applauding for me and from time to time saying, "Well done, my child," is a tremendous motivator for me to live a godly life.

Maybe you get discouraged. You say, "I've been trying to do the right thing in my marriage, but I don't see any results." You say, "I've been trying to respond correctly to my kids or to my parents—or to my spouse—but it doesn't seem to make a difference." You say, "I've been trying to have a good testimony at work or school, and I just don't know that it's paying off. Frankly, I don't see it making any impact in anybody's life." But God's applauding and saying, "I see it. And no good thing will ever go unrewarded from me."

Galatians 6:9 says, "Let us not become weary in doing good, for at the proper time we will reap a harvest if we do not give up." So hang in there. God is rejoicing when you do the right thing.

God Rejoices When We Give Our Lives to Jesus Christ

Look at Luke 15:10, "There is rejoicing in the presence of the angels of God over one sinner who repents." That's saying when you turn your life to Jesus Christ, Heaven breaks out into a great big party for you. God smiles and God rejoices because that which was lost is found. He can extend to you so many things that he's wanted to extend to you when you give your life to Christ:

• Forgiveness of your sin.
• The presence of the Holy Spirit in your life.
• The promise of eternal life.
• And he welcomes you home with the same joy and emotion with which a parent welcomes home a long lost child.

Friend, God personally put himself through a lot of hurt for you on the cross so he could save you. That's what he wants and is ready to do. But God never makes that choice for you. He extends to you the opportunity, but you have to respond.

If you want God to extend to you his divine assistance to help heal your hidden hurts, you need to come to Christ if you haven't already. This book has been addressed primarily to those who are already in Christ. You cannot receive all the benefits I have described without having a relationship with him.

So if you haven't already, why don't you turn your life over to God today? God knows you, loves you, sent his Son Jesus Christ to die for you, and he brought you into contact with these pages for a purpose today. You are not reading this book by accident. God knew you needed these words today. Think about it: God knew you would be reading these words on this day before you were even born.

This could even be your day of salvation (2 Corinthians 6:2b). Why wait another day? (See Acts 22:16.) Following Christ is the most logical, rational, intelligent thing you will ever do. Don't wait one more minute to get in touch with the One who made you. Open up your heart to him today and experience his saving love.

————

Questions for Discussion

1. Have you ever before associated the normal emotions of parenthood with God? How does the recognition that God has such feelings make you feel? What action does it encourage you to take?

2. Of the emotions cited by the author under the heading, "God Has Emotions, Too," which was most surprising to you? Why? What emotions would you have added if you had been making the list? Why?

3. Most people, like the author, are especially careful not to do things that might grieve their parents. Why do you think we are not as careful about grieving our Heavenly Father? How would we act if we were?

4. The author cites 1 Peter 5:7: "Cast all you anxiety on him because he cares for you." Have you ever prayed with the intention of casting your anxiety on the Lord, but found later you were still carrying a good bit of it yourself? How does one release his anxieties to the Lord? How can Christian brothers and sisters help?

5. If God has plans for us "to prosper" (Jeremiah 29:11), why is it some Christians never seem to prosper?

6. The author says worry is "the result of not recognizing the omniscience of God." Do you agree or disagree? How

can we develop the character to worry less and trust God more?

7. According to the author, "You don't pray to tell God your needs; you pray to show you're trusting him." What are some other reasons we pray?

8. Hebrews 6:10 links helping people with showing love to God. Name some specific acts you can do for people that would show love for God and bring him joy.

9. The author says, "It's your character, not your reputation, that is important." Do you agree or disagree? Why? How does Proverbs 22:1 relate to this issue? "A good name [reputation] is more desirable than great riches. . . ."

10. Have you given your life to Jesus Christ? If not, discuss the idea with a Christian friend. Isn't it time you did so?